Galapagos: *through writers' eyes*

Galapagos:

The Enchanted Islands

through writers' eyes

JOHN HICKMAN

updated by Julian Fitter

ELAND
London

First published by Anthony Nelson in 1985
First published by Eland Publishing Limited in 2009
61 Exmouth Market, London EC1R 4QL

Text © John Hickman 1985

ISBN 978 1906011 10 9

Text set by Nick Randall
Cover Image: Marine Iguana on Beach © Mark Karrass/Corbis

Contents

Acknowledgements to 1985 edition

I acknowledge with great gratitude my debt to Mr G. T. Corley Smith, formerly Secretary-General of the Charles Darwin Foundation, and one of the prime movers in establishing its conservation and scientific work in the Galapagos. He generously gave me full and unconditional use of his own work covering much of the ground included in this book and produced the original drafts for Chapter 16 and the Appendix based on his special knowledge of the islands and the Foundation. Nevertheless, the responsibility for any errors of fact or opinion is entirely mine.

I have also been much helped and encouraged in various ways by Mr Julian Fitter, who lived many years in the Galapagos and knows more about them than I ever shall. He helped with comments and original material for several chapters and provided many of the photographs. Others were kindly provided by Mr Roger Perry. Sr Miguel Cifuentes, Head of the Galapagos National Park Service, also commented most helpfully on Chapter 16.

Acknowledgements to 2009 edition

The publishers would like to thank Julian Fitter for reading the final chapters of the book and updating the information therein.

FOR JENNY

Preface

I**T WAS FIFTY** years ago that my father saw the Galapagos Islands for the first time. In 1959, before I was born, he and my mother were on a six-week sea voyage to New Zealand, their first diplomatic posting, when their ship passed close to the islands; and as he later recalled, 'we speculated about the strange inhabitants which had inspired Darwin's theories of the origin of species.'

It was not for another twenty years, however, towards the end of his career, that he was able to visit the islands for himself. In 1978, as the British Ambassador to Ecuador, my father went to the Galapagos to pay an official call on the Govenor of the Archipelago de Colon, a province of the country; unofficially he was there for an Easter holiday with his wife and family. I was then seventeen, my brothers Matthew and Andrew fourteen and twelve.

Tourism in the Galapagos – if you could call it that at all – barely existed in 1978. Although it was by then possible to arrive by air, the airfield on Baltra Island consisted of a landing strip with a tin shack at one end, and a man whose job it was (can this really have been true ?) to frighten off the goats when they strayed too near the tarmac.

With only a fraction of the number of visitors that there are today, there were far fewer restrictions then on which islands you could visit or where you could walk, although even in those days it was obligatory to take an official guide. Ours was an extremely handsome young marine biologist, David Whyte, who not only knew everything there was to know about frigate birds, marine iguanas and the mating dance of the giant albatross, but who wrote poetry in his spare time and shared my love of Donne's metaphysical verse (I was revising for my Engish A-levels at the time. Truly, that Easter week, God was in his heaven for my seventeen-year-old self, and all was right with the world.)

We had rented a small yacht, *The Bronzewing*, and it was from this that Dad paid his official visit. We arrived at the Governor's headquarters in Puerto Baquerizo, to be met and taken ashore in his barge – 'an elderly lighter' as Dad was later to recall with characteristic relish 'normally used for transporting cement'. Spruced up for the occasion in our least crumpled t-shirts (what on earth did my father wear? A suit and cocked hat? Surely not...), we all sat huddling in the shade of the Governor's corrugated iron porch, sipping lukewarm Sprite and watching with fascination as a shark's fin slowly circled the boat we had just left behind in the bay.

Part of the allure of the Galapagos, then as now, is that it is full of such small adventures. For my father, always a romantic, this was certainly some of their appeal. Once formalities with the Governor, such as they were, had been completed, we were free 'to sail into the empty archipelago,' as he later recalled. 'For a week at a time, we saw no other people and very few signs of humanity and we experienced every day that feeling of harmony with the natural world which is the greatest reward of travel in wild places.'

But, actually, with the benefit of hindsight it is clear that it was always the human stories that most appealed to Dad. He was entranced, of course, as we all were, by the Garden-of-Eden quality of the islands and their unique wildlife; the wilderness experience however – no hot showers for a week, and fried plantains, which he abominated, for breakfast, lunch, tea and dinner – was not really his thing. But those stories about buccaneers, Swiss Family Robinsons and, most especially, pirates (this was a man, after all, whose own eccentric childhood was not unlike something out of Arthur Ransome's *Swallows and Amazons*) – now they were really something and were, of course, the inspiration for this book. He would have been chuffed to bits to know that after twenty-five years Eland are bringing it back into print.

I have two family photograph albums beside me as I write this. One shows that Easter week back in 1978; the other a second visit we made to the Galapagos in 2005, when, four years after my father died, my mother took our now extended family back there on a holiday.

They say you should never go back. This second trip was altogether a more sophisticated affair. No Governor, no cement barge; a proper airport on Baltra now, souvenirs, shops. The photographs show that we are all wearing wet suits in the water; no more stripey, school flannel pyjamas (my mother's brainwave) to protect us from the sun. Not a fried plantain in sight. Although it can no longer be described as an 'empty archipelago', the peculiar magic of the Galapagos remains.

The last of the photographs shows a group picture taken at sunset one day. My mother; her three children – a little stouter, a little more faded at the edges now, all of us, it must be said; and new additions in the form of a daughter- and son-in-law, six grandchildren. Twelve of us in all: windswept, sunburned, gritty-haired, grinning. Impossible to believe that if I look a little harder I won't see Dad smiling out at me too.

Katie Hickman
London, 2008

Introduction

THE GALAPAGOS ISLANDS rise out of the Great South Sea, which the Spaniards found when they crossed the Isthmus of Panama and looked out from their 'peak in Darien' across the wide Pacific. They are tropical islands, lying across the equator itself, but were desert in 1485 when they were first discovered and remained deserted for another three centuries. Lying 960 kilometres from the western coast of South America in the empty Pacific Ocean, they are too remote and inhospitable to have attracted any permanent settlers in all those years. We know of them largely from the diaries and recollections of mariners, pirates, privateers, whalers, explorers and naval men who visited the archipelago, voluntarily or involuntarily, at irregular intervals. For them the Galapagos provided the only anchorage and source of supply in that vast area of ocean. The Spaniards who came there in the sixteenth century called them Las Islas Encantadas (the Enchanted Islands), and the visionary American author, Herman Melville, used that name as the title for his book. But Melville saw them as arid and even sinister:

> Take five and twenty heaps of cinders dumped here and there in an outside lot; imagine some of them magnified into mountains and the vacant lot the sea; and you will have a fit idea of the general aspect of the Encantadas.

What then is their enchantment? All islands attract men strongly because they are safe havens from the perils of the sea and, perhaps, because they are worlds apart and easier, if only through their smallness, for us to comprehend. The Galapagos Islands certainly appear out of this world, moonscapes unchanged since primeval times except by the lava flowing from newly-erupting volcanoes. While seemingly easier to know and understand, these islands are, in fact, an unpredictable wilderness filled with an extraordinary population of unique species and subspecies, which have developed apart from humans and their dominating influence.

For the vast majority of the known history of the Galapagos, it was hard for people to reach the islands, and harder still to survive on them. Since 1945 access has become easier and considerable numbers of tourists can stay for as long as they want. The United States unlocked the door to the islands in Word War II by the construction of a military airstrip on Seymour Island. This has now been taken over by the Republic of Ecuador as the base for the development of a tourist industry and a vital channel for essential supplies. Those who visit the islands today will probably arrive first at Baltra airfield on Seymour and sleep in comfortable ships or guest houses ashore. They come to see the giant tortoises (in Spanish *galapagos*), the marine and land iguanas, the flightless cormorants, albatrosses and penguins, and the many other extraordinary creatures which Charles Darwin first observed in detail one hundred and fifty years ago.

The natural history of 'Darwin's Islands' has been described in many books. Few of them dwell much on the strange and haunted lives of the men, and occasionally women, who made their history. This book tries to put the Galapagos archipelago into a human perspective recognisable to the armchair traveller as well as the professional naturalist. Its purpose is to describe the human history: what men have done to the islands and the effect they have had on man himself.

1

The Inca's Tale

THE GALAPAGOS ARCHIPELAGO is one of the few places on the Earth where aborigines never existed, and their absence partly explains the extraordinary way in which other animal life was able to develop there. The islands have been known to Europeans for 450 years, but no permanent settlement took place until well into the nineteenth century. The early history of the Galapagos is known to us, therefore, only through the written records left by a succession of visitors who stayed briefly and left nothing behind them. But the few men who did come, like Charles Darwin in 1835, were all remarkable in their own ways.

Until recent times no one could arrive at the islands without a share of adventuring spirit and luck – in some cases bad luck. These visitors have been the *dramatis personae* in a series of comedies, tragedies and mysteries which it would be hard to match. These islands, more than most, have attracted strange people and have seen ordinary people forced into strange circumstances. Often this was because life has never been something to take for granted in the Galapagos. Only people who have had a strong motive have come to them on purpose, and only the single-minded have stayed for long. The strongest deterrent has usually been the lack of reliable supplies of fresh water, and after that the lack of cultivable land. In the earliest days some believed that these were rich and fruitful islands to be sought and enjoyed by the fortunate. Even when all the known evidence proved the opposite, plenty of blind optimists continued to trust idyllic myths. However, even those who left disappointed knew that they had found something remarkable.

The first visitors were sailors from the Chimu culture, which was centred on the coast of northern Peru and flourished there just before the height of Inca power. We know of their contact with the Galapagos purely from potsherds found there and identified by Thor Heyerdahl. They probably did not stay long but these remnants confirm that people from the mainland visited the islands before the Spaniards came. There are also reasons to believe that one of the greatest Incas, Tupac Yupanqui, came himself or sent an expedition to the Galapagos in about 1485, the year that the first of the Tudors, Henry VII, won the English crown at Bosworth Field.

Topa Yupanqui was the Inca king at the height of that nation's formidable power, from about 1471 to 1493. One of the greatest historians of the period, Pedro Sarmiento de Gamboa, writing in about 1570 told a story which Spanish conquistadors had heard many times since they arrived in Peru in 1524:

> When Topa Yupanqui had conquered the coast of Manta, the island of Puna and Tumbez (Ecuador and northern Peru), some traders arrived by sea from further west in balsas (rafts) with sails. They told him that they had come from two islands called Avachumbi and Nina-chumbi, where there were many people and much gold.

At first the Inca refused to believe the story 'because merchants were people who talked a lot'. So he called in a man named Antarqui, whom he always took with him on his campaigns as a personal necromancer and who could fly through the air. Antarqui made a reconnaissance and confirmed to the Inca that he had seen the islands with all their people and wealth.

So Topa Inka, with this certain knowledge, decided to go there. And for this he made a great quantity of balsas and embarked 20,000 picked soldiers in them. Topa Inka sailed away, discovered the islands and on his return brought with him some black men, much gold, a chair made of brass, and the skin and jawbone of a horse. These trophies were kept in the fortress at Cuzco until the time of the Spaniards.

It would be easy to regard all this as a fairy story. Dismissing the airborne magician and the mighty invasion force of twenty thousand seaborne soldiers as predictable traveller's tales, what of the Inca's strange trophies? There were no black people, gold, brass nor horses in the Galapagos. Indeed, there were none in the whole of South America before the Spanish Conquest. This story is not the first to have been elaborated in the telling and improved in a way likely to appeal to the Spaniards to whom it was told. The conquistadors wanted to hear of exotic wealth and the Incas were keen to oblige. On the other hand, the meaning of Nina-chumbi is 'island of fire', while Avachumbi means 'island beyond'. The Inca informants of Pedro Sarmiento would hardly have been likely to invent a story of volcanic islands unless they had some direct knowledge of such islands. There are plenty of volcanoes in the high Andes of Ecuador, but these were much less accessible from the coast than offshore islands in the eastern Pacific. It is much more likely that coastal dwellers would have heard of the Galapagos as 'islands of fire' in the ocean.

It was once thought that balsa rafts could not sail such distances, but Thor Heyerdahl proved otherwise in his celebrated voyage in the *Kon-Tiki*. He wrote:

I have during recent experiments in Ecuador rediscovered the lost Peruvian and Ecuadorian art of centre-board navigation. With correct use of centre-boards, such as are historically and archaeologically known from Peru and Ecuador, the large aboriginal balsa can sail and tack into the wind, and it is abundantly clear that the range to and from the Galapagos was fully within the capacity of the aboriginal cultures of the north-west coast of South America.

Another objection is that the pre-Columbian civilisations had no knowledge of astronomy and, therefore, no method of navigation out of sight of land. This argument can cut the other way because pre-Columbian sailors would be unlikely for that very reason to seek to reach remote and unknown lands. They would only venture to places already known which they could have some hope of finding again and the Galapagos were already known to Topa Inka from the stories of wandering merchants, people of his own tribe or a tribe well known to him.

However, what seems to settle the issue is the fact that anyone setting sail from the coast of Ecuador in a primitive ship is quite likely to end up in the Galapagos whether they intend to or not. Centre-board rafts are not very manoeuvrable in the best of conditions, and no sailing vessel can be relied on to hold a course when the wind fails, as it often does in tropical latitudes. For most of the year, the cold Humboldt current which sweeps up the west coasts of Chile and Peru from the Antarctic carries everything with it remorselessly in a long arc towards the Galapagos. It would have been surprising indeed if rafts had not quite often been carried away from the coast by this current and, however unwillingly, reached the islands.

Pedro Sarmiento de Gamboa was one of the outstanding explorers, navigators and historians of the Spanish conquest of Peru. He was the first navigator to pass through the Straits of Magellan from west to east, in the course of efforts to counter the first penetration of Sir Francis Drake into the Pacific in about 1580, and he charted the sea passages south of the continent. According to Sir Walter Raleigh, he earned the reputation in England (where he spent time as a prisoner of war) of being both a great gentleman and a scientist and scholar. At the same time, like Raleigh, he had the soaring imagination of an optimist and romantic. He had long believed that the islands visited by the Inca in the previous century were not only rich in themselves but were also the outposts of other lands in the Pacific, perhaps even a great new continent to the south-west. After years of putting pressure on all who would listen, it seemed in 1567 that Sarmiento had finally succeeded in organising an expedition to discover these fabulous new territories. The Governor of Peru agreed to send two ships, the *Los Reyes* of 250 tons and the *Todos Santos* of 107 tons, with full crews of soldiers and sailors, to find these lands.

However, to Sarmiento's fury the Governor gave the command to his own nephew, Alvaro de Mendaña. The much-chagrined instigator of the voyage had to be content with the role of captain of the larger ship. According to Sarmiento's own report sent to King Philip II five years later, the expedition did rediscover the islands of Avachumbi and Nina-chumbi but the commander (Mendaña) refused to land there because he wished to return later and claim all credit for the discovery himself. It was no consolation to Sarmiento that the expedition went on across the Pacific and there discovered the Solomon Islands. This was a more significant achievement because the only rich and productive lands in the Pacific Ocean are nearer to the western side, and there are none of any great intrinsic wealth as near as the Galapagos.

Being as far removed as we are from the Spanish conquest of America, it is difficult, perhaps impossible, to disentangle fact from myth. In his effort to establish the truth, Sarmiento tested the story of the Inca's journey to the islands of Avachumbi and Nina-chumbi by having his manuscript translated and read out to a group of fifty Inca notables and members of the royal line who confirmed that it was true. Then, as now, the Andean people were no doubt liable to answer any question put to them with the reply which they thought the questioner hoped to hear; but this does not necessarily invalidate their evidence completely. It is in fact very probable that an outstandingly adventurous ruler of an expanding civilisation, like Topa Yupanqui, should have made a pioneering voyage into the Eastern Pacific and discovered one, or possibly more than one, group of offshore islands. There are not many islands within navigable distance of the coast of the Inca empire and the Galapagos, being the largest such group, were the most likely to be discovered. They could quite well have been the ones discovered by Inca travellers or by the Inca himself. Moreover if the Inca's courtiers and chroniclers were inclined to exaggerate the importance of the trophies he acquired on his travels, it would not be the first or the last example of flattering a king.

And, if Inca rafts could reach the Galapagos, it would be hard indeed to deny the possibility that Pedro Sarmiento de Gamboa had followed them there.

It is uncertain whether Pedro de Sarmiento truly achieved his life's ambition to find the islands 'where Topa Inka Yupanqui went'. He placed them about 200 hundred leagues (about 950 kilometres) from Lima and 14 degrees south of the equator. As an expert navigator he could not conceivably have calculated the position of the Galapagos as being 14 degrees south; nor could he have placed the Solomons or any other western Pacific islands so near to the South American coast. Thor Heyerdahl believed that the islands which Sarmiento was prevented from claiming personally must have been in the Easter Island group, and these are, indeed, closest to where he thought he had found the Inca's treasure islands.

2

The Bishop's Tale

LONG BEFORE SARMIENTO'S VOYAGE, but only seven years after the Inca's alleged discovery of two islands in the archipelago, another event had taken place in Europe which was to change the course of history in the New World. After centuries of campaigning, the liberation of Spain from the Moors was finally assured in 1492 when Granada opened its gates to the 'Catholic kings', Ferdinand and Isabela. In the same year, they authorised Columbus's first westward voyage and he made his first landfall in the Caribbean. Columbus's later discoveries on the mainland of South America opened the doors of the New World to an influx of adventuring soldiers of fortune, whose energies had previously been absorbed in the campaigns against the Moors.

These voyages were undertaken first and foremost in the name of the kings of Spain for the conversion of heathen souls. Ironically, the whole enterprise was blessed by Alexander VI, the Borgia pope, who divided the New World for this purpose between Spain and Portugal. The fact that the conquistadors were often more strongly motivated by lust for gold, while the Spanish crown took one fifth of all the wealth found in the Americas, does not detract from the sincerity of the evangelical purpose shared by the Church, the monarchy and even Columbus himself. For centuries Europe, and Spain in particular, had been threatened by militant Islam. Less than forty years previously Constantinople had been captured, and most of Spain had been in Arab hands for seven centuries or more. The resurgence of the Christian faith and its military vanguard of Spanish *tercios* tipped the balance of power in Europe decisively at the end of the fifteenth century. These forces were then directed outwards and they reaped great rewards in the New World in the first half of the sixteenth century. In 1532, Francisco Pizarro captured the Inca King Atahualpa, grandson of Tupac Yupanqui, extorted a huge quantity of treasure from him, and after only three years had all but subjugated the Inca empire. This was an extraordinary achievement, which was accomplished only by unparalleled courage and military skill combined with total ruthlessness. Not surprisingly, such men rapidly fell out with one another, and Pizarro was soon in conflict with his lieutenant and chief partner, Diego de Almagro.

King Charles V and the Council of the Indies in Spain were familiar with the problem but, half a world away, had little means of controlling quarrelsome commanders. Since the first discoveries, the conquistadors had all too often fought each other and, quite contrary to their instructions, been quick to exploit, ill-treat and enslave the conquered natives for their own gain. In 1529 Pizarro had been authorised to discover and conquer this new territory, and been named Governor and Captain-General of Peru. The king now called in the Bishop of Panama, Fray Tomás de Berlanga, in whose diocese lay all the known and unknown Spanish territories in the Americas. Fray Tomás was ordered to go to Peru, report on the territories which had been conquered in the king's name, investigate the situation which had arisen between the conquistador leaders, and, in particular, look into the Governor's treatment of the Indians, which was to be improved and moderated.

This was a tall order for anyone to undertake single-handedly, but since Charles was Holy Roman Emperor and ruler of most of Austria, Italy, Germany, France, Belgium and the Netherlands in addition to Spain and the Americas, he was not likely to think his orders to Fray Tomás unduly heavy. Tomás was probably not surprised to be ordered on a mission which was more political than spiritual. He had been Prior of the Dominican Order in Hispaniola since 1508 and then Provincial of the Order throughout the New World. In 1528 he was also appointed the third Bishop of Castilla del Oro, as Panama was then called. In that capacity he had, perhaps, the greatest authority in the entire continent.

Following his instructions precisely, he procured or built a caravel, assembled a crew, supplies and a complement of horses, and set sail on February 23rd, 1535. For seven days the winds held and the Bishop's ship made progress towards the equator. They sailed, as was usual at that time, sufficiently inshore to use coastal landmarks for navigation. But on the eighth day flat calm descended and the sails hung limp and unmoving. Without the least breath of wind to help them control it, the boat began to drift further out to sea into the unknown waters of the Pacific Ocean. Every day the anxious crew gazed round the horizon, but saw not a cloud or hint of rain, only the fiery sun and sky, and the flat surface of the sea as the land disappeared completely to the east. Men and horses were beginning to suffer from both heat and thirst when on Wednesday March 10th they sighted an island. Fray Tomás reported the whole story to the king in a despatch written in Puerto Viejo (Ecuador) when he finally got back there a month later.

Your Imperial Catholic Majesty   6 April 1535
It seems eminently correct to me to allow Your Majesty to know of the progress of my trip from the time when I left Panama, which was on 23 February of the current year, until I arrived in this new town of Puerto Viejo.

The ship sailed with very good breezes for seven days, and the pilot kept near land and we had a six-day calm; the currents were so strong and engulfed us in such a way that on Wednesday 10 March we sighted an island. As on board there was enough water for only two more days, they agreed to lower the lifeboat and go on land for water and grass for the horses. Once out, they found nothing but seals, and turtles, and such big tortoises that each could carry a man on top of itself, and many iguanas that are like serpents. On another day, we saw another island, larger than the first, and with great sierras. Thinking that, on account of its size and monstrous shape, there could not fail to be rivers and fruits, we went to it, because the distance around the first one was about four or five leagues, and around the other ten or twelve leagues. At this juncture the water on the ship gave out and we were three days in reaching the island on account of the calms, during which all of us, as well as the horses, suffered great hardship.

The boat once anchored, we all went on land, and some were given charge of making a well, and others of looking over the island. From the well there came out water saltier than that of the sea. On land they were not able to find even a drop of water for two days, and with the thirst the people felt, they resorted to a leaf of some thistles like prickly pears, and because they were somewhat juicy, although not very tasty, we began to eat of them and squeeze them to draw all the water from them and then drank it as if it were rose water.

On Passion Sunday, I had them bring on land the things necessary for saying Mass, and after it was said I again sent the people in twos and threes, over different paths. The Lord deigned that they should find in a ravine among the rocks as much as a hogshead of water, and after they had drawn that, they found more and more. Finally, eight hogsheads were filled and the barrels and the jugs that were there on the boat, but through the lack of water we lost one man, and two days after we had left that island we lost another; and ten horses died.

From this island, we saw two others, one much larger than all which was easily fifteen or twenty leagues around; the other was medium. I took the latitude to know where the islands were, and they are between a half-degree and a degree-and-a-half south latitude. On this second one, the same conditions prevailed as on the first; many seals, turtles, iguanas, tortoises, many birds like those of Spain, but so silly that they do not know how to flee, and many were caught in the hand. The other two islands we did not touch; I do not know their character. On this one, on the sands of the shore, there were some small stones that we stepped on as we landed, and there were diamond-like stones and others amber-coloured. But on the whole island, I do not think that there is a place where one might sow a bushel of corn, because most of it is full of very big stones, so much so, that it seems as though sometime God had showered stones; and the earth there is like dross, worthless, because it has not the power of raising a little grass, but only some thistles, the leaf of which I said we picked. Thinking that we were not more than twenty or thirty leagues from this soil of Peru, we were satisfied with the water already mentioned, although we might have filled more of our casks. But we set sail, and with medium weather we sailed eleven days without sighting land, and the pilot and the master of the ship came to me to ask where we were and to tell me there was only one hogshead of water on the ship. I tried to take the altitude of the sun that day and found that we were three degrees south latitude, and I realised that with the directions we were taking, we were becoming more and more engulfed, that we were not heading for land, because we were sailing south; I had them tack on the other side, and the hogshead of water I had divided as follows: half was given for the animals and with the other half a beverage was made which was put into the wine cask, for I held it as certain that we could not be far from land, and we sailed for eight days, all of which the hogshead of the beverage lasted, by giving a ration to each one with which he was satisfied. And when that hogshead gave out and there was no relief for us, we sighted land and we had calm for two days, during which we drank only wine, but we took heart on sighting land. We entered the bay and river of the Caraques (in Ecuador)

17

on Friday 9 April, and we met there the people of a galleon from Nicaragua who had left eight months before, so we considered our trip good in comparison with theirs . . .

Like all the early visitors to the Galapagos, Fray Tomás and his companions arrived thirsty; and, like most of them, they came involuntarily. The Bishop seems to have been of a practical rather than an imaginative cast of mind. He was impressed, naturally enough, with the size of the tortoises but he recorded this with little emotion, and noted the tameness of the birds but attributed this to their silliness. He neither claimed nor gave any name to his discovery but we know that the great Flemish cartographer, Abraham Ortelius, heard of the islands from this despatch and the pilot's report on the voyage. Ortelius seems to have been the first to name them and he showed them as 'Isolas de Galapagos' in his *Orbis Terrarum* published in 1574. This is the only evidence that the Bishop's discovery made any impact at all. In Spain far more important and valuable matters were being reported from the mainland and elsewhere at the time, and the despatch lay virtually untouched in the archives in Seville until it was finally published in a collection of unedited documents in 1883 in Madrid.

When he finally got to Lima, Bishop Berlanga issued various ordinances in favour of the Indians, and requested Pizarro to take particular care of the safety of the Inca whom he had chosen to replace the murdered Atahualpa. The cold-blooded and unjustified execution by garrotting of Atahualpa had been greeted with much criticism in Spain and the Bishop openly berated Pizarro for it. Later he had to report to the king that Pizarro had shown himself totally unreceptive to all arguments and he eventually returned to Panama with little accomplished despite the great dangers and hardships he had met with on his mission. A year later, Berlanga resigned his bishopric and retired to Spain.

Ten years after this inadvertent discovery of the Galapagos, another brave man arrived in even stranger circumstances. The bitter feuding between the conquistadors had become outright war. In 1546, one of the few faithful defenders of the royal cause, Diego Centeño, was defeated in battle in southern Peru and forced to flee from Gonzalo Pizarro's field commander, Francisco Carvajal, known to his enemies as the 'demon of the Andes'. To prepare their departure by sea, Centeño sent one of his officers, Diego de Rivadeneira, ahead to Arica, on what is now the border between Chile and Peru. With a group of twelve soldiers and a few impressed sailors, Rivadeneira sailed to the meeting place arranged with Centeño at Quilca. However, the latter was by that time so closely pursued by Carvajal, whose reputation for cruelty and bloodthirstiness was unequalled even in that barbarous age, that he dared not wait for the ship and fled into the mountains.

When Diego de Rivadeneira reached Quilca he, too, only narrowly escaped capture by the terrible Carvajal, and made off by sea to the north, keeping well out of sight of land. After twenty-five days they turned in towards the coast again and sighted land. Concluding with panic that it was the coast of northern Peru, well within reach of Pizarro's ships, they quickly turned east again, in spite of having very little food left. Eventually they sighted a large island 'which always seemed to be covered by a cloud, which had many inlets but even so had high mountains near the coast: some said they saw smoke (rising from them) and others said not'.

Rivadeneira and his pitiful crew had fled in such haste that they had no maps, compass or pilot, and so they could not fix the position of this island. The smoke rising from the mountain peaks is unmistakably a description of a volcano. The contemporary historian who gave the best account of this voyage, Pedro Cieza de León, also recounted that on another island where the group landed they found great numbers of sea-lions, tortoises, iguanas and birds. There seems little question that the Galapagos had been accidentally discovered again.

They saw twelve or thirteen other islands but landed only once. Cieza de León describes it: 'As they had little water and realised they were not as near Nicaragua as they had previously thought, they set out in different directions to look for some water. But each fearing that he would be left behind by the others, they soon came back to the shore and re-embarked to continue on their way very sadly because of their lack of food and water.' He adds smugly that 'it seems to me that if they had calmly sought water they would have found it.' Cieza de León did not know the Galapagos.

Continuing their voyage northwards, Rivadeneira and his crew suffered horribly from thirst and hunger. A large turtle floated alongside, and one young man climbed on to it to capture it. Unfortunately, through some unexpected change of wind or current, the ship drifted away into the distance leaving the boy, who could not swim, sitting astride his turtle until exhaustion overtook him. The others managed to keep alive on the flesh of sharks and other fish, which they caught with harpoons made from their spurs. After four days without a drop of water, they finally landed at San José de Istapa in Guatemala.

The only official account of Diego de Rivadeneira's 'discovery' of the archipelago is given in a letter which the Royal Treasurer of Guatemala, Francisco de Castellanos, sent to king Philip II on August 27th, 1546. As Castellanos unkindly put it, he would give the king an account of 'the journey made by that unwilling mariner and explorer-by-accident'.

Diego de Rivadeneira, one of Centeño's captains, fled in a small boat with twelve or fifteen soldiers towards another province. On his way he found an island near the coast where he spent three days. It is below the equator with a high profile and big mountains and said to be eighty leagues in circumference. He landed on another island near the first where he found tortoises, turtles, iguanas, sea-lions, birds called flamencos, doves and other birds, among them a beautiful gyrfalcon which has never been seen here (in Central America) or I believe in Peru, although there are falcons there. Near this island there are ten or twelve other small ones.

One would have thought that Rivadeneira, having all but died of thirst on his involuntary expedition, would have been thankful to see the last of those inhospitable islands. However he and his kind were a tough and determined breed of adventurer, whose optimism and appetite for power and wealth were insatiable. He petitioned the king for authority to colonise and govern an archipelago about which he knew very little more than that it had no fresh water. There is no record of any reply from Spain, and perhaps it was lucky for Don Diego that he never had reason to return.

There are scattered references in the Spanish chronicles of the latter part of the sixteenth century to other sightings of islands which may have been the Galapagos. Apart from the Cocos Islands, 640 kilometres north-east and lying between Galapagos and Panama, there are practically no other islands anywhere near the western coast of South America, so any islands found within navigable distance of the coast probably were the Galapagos. Again, it is not easy to tell fact from fiction in the tales told to the historians of the time. Pedro Cieza de León, for example, whets the appetite of his readers with an account of 'very big islands populated by rich people with lots of gold and silver, and well provided with fruit trees and many other good things. They say that these people come to trade on the mainland in big piraguas and canoes.' Another historian tells of a lay member of the Dominican order, Fray Martín Barragán, 'a hell-fire preacher and the terror of sinners, steady in virtue and a great penitent', who was shipwrecked for three years in the Galapagos and underwent his conversion there. When we find that a well-known navigator of the time placed the islands east-south-east of the island of La Plata, near Manta on the coast of Ecuador, and 100 leagues (480 kilometres) from Paita on the Peruvian coast, we can only conclude that the fiery preacher Barragán, and anyone else shipwrecked in the Galapagos in those days, was more than lucky to be found again.

3

Out of the Mists

THE INCAS, THE BISHOP and the would-be-conquistadors may have reached the islands but they never truly discovered them. At best they touched the volcanic shores of one or two islands and passed on knowing scarcely any more than when they arrived. Except for Fray Tomás de Berlanga, none left any reliable account of where he had been or what he had seen, so the pictures we have of these visits are the shadowy images of myth rather than the clear outlines of history.

Until 1574 when the name of Galapagos first appears, the islands were usually known to their Spanish visitors as Las Encantadas, the Enchanted or Bewitched Islands. It seems to have been Diego de Rivadeneira who gave them this name because of the strong and capricious currents which so often prevented sailing boats from landing. Even today fishing boats are sometimes lost forever in passage from one part of the archipelago to another. It is not surprising that the first visitors, with primitive sailing capacity, believed that it was not the ships but the islands themselves that were drifting, and land which was liable to recede and disappear from human view must be enchanted. This reputation was no doubt embroidered and magnified over the years. However, once the islands had been placed on a map and named after their most famous inhabitants by Abraham Ortelius they became part of the known world and not only places of legend and myth. What then were they really like?

The most meticulous eye that ever sighted the islands was that of Charles Darwin. In his diary for September 16th, 1835 he wrote:

These islands at a distance have a sloping uniform outline, excepting where broken by sundry paps and hillocks; the whole black lava, completely covered by small leafless brushwood and low trees. The fragments of lava, where most porous, are reddish like cinders; the stunted trees show little signs of life. The black rocks heated by the rays of the vertical sun, like a stove, give to the air a close and sultry feeling. The plants also smell unpleasantly. The country was comparable to what one might imagine the cultivated parts of the Infernal regions to be.

Captain Fitzroy of HMS *Beagle*, in which Darwin arrived, summed up the aspect of the coast more succinctly as 'a fit shore for Pandemonium'. This is the overwhelming impression which today's visitor gets on first approaching the coast from the sea – a preview of purgatory rather than a glimpse of paradise. There were some features which Darwin could not see or did not notice on his first arrival, but he noticed the all-pervading fact that the islands are entirely volcanic in origin.

The archipelago lies across the equator enclosed in an area of about 60,000 square kilometres, and the easternmost island, Chatham, is about 960 kilometres west of the coast of the republic of Ecuador. The total land area is about 7,800 square kilometres, the largest island, Albemarle, being about 120 kilometres long and somewhat greater in area than all the others put together.

There are four other fairly large islands (Narborough, James, Santa Cruz and Chatham), ten or a dozen smaller ones (depending on what is defined as an island) and many rocks and islets. With the exception of the two northernmost islands, Culpepper and Wenman, all of them rise from a relatively shallow submarine shelf

– the Galapagos Platform – which is 370 to 900 metres below the surface and over 1,800 metres above the ocean floor. The central area between Narborough and Chatham is nearly all less than 180 metres deep and contains all the larger islands.

Albemarle consists of six separate volcanoes, five of which are typical shield volcanoes with immense summit calderas (collapsed craters), one being eight kilometres in diameter. The other islands, with the exception of Chatham, consist of a single large volcano and its subsidiaries, and the biggest volcanoes rise to over 1,500 metres. Until recently that on Narborough had a great crater over 900 metres deep with a lake in the floor and, rising out of the lake, a smaller crater which contained another lake. During the last great eruption in 1968 the floor of the larger crater collapsed another 300 metres, the lake reformed on the opposite side and the cone of the smaller crater was breached, so that the water drained away.

The islands are of major importance geologically and are regarded as one of the most active volcanic fields in the world. There are two conflicting schools of thought among scientists about the geological history and physical origin of the Galapagos. Although it is not necessary to go into the details of this controversy, we need to understand something of it if we are to see how if affects the theory of biological evolution.

Some geologists believe that the archipelago was once connected to the American mainland by a land-bridge which later subsided. For example, there have been speculations about a land-bridge via the Cocos Islands to Costa Rica or via the Carnegie Ridge to Ecuador. Others hold that the islands have never been part of any other land mass but erupted directly from the ocean bed through volcanic activity. The latter opinion is now the more widely accepted, and it is itself divided into two subsidiary streams of thought. One argues that a sizeable land mass, originating separately from the continent, has partially subsided, leaving only the present group of islands above the surface. The other view, which Darwin also maintained, is that the islands of today are the result of entirely separate volcanic building processes and were never connected with each other.

The significance of this for the evolution of life on the islands is whether the fauna and flora came gradually to the Galapagos over about 960 uninterrupted kilometres of ocean; or arrived across a land-bridge or by way of the stepping stones which existed if and when the islands were part of a larger separate landmass.

More importantly for biologists, the seeds and animal organisms, however they arrived in the Galapagos islands, have developed there in an isolated and oceanic environment. This geographical isolation and remoteness are the crucial elements determining the Galapagoan environment, and explain why the archipelago is called a laboratory of evolution. It provides conditions in which species can adapt without competing or interbreeding with their continental precursors.

The resulting evolutionary divergence found on these islands is unmatched elsewhere – relatives of the sunflower which have evolved into trees; gulls which forage at night; lizards which feed on seaweed beneath the sea; tortoises which weigh 230 kilograms; and cormorants which cannot fly. The Galapagos plants and animals are mostly related to the species found in North, South and Central America as well as the West Indies. This fact is sometimes used by the 'land-bridge' or 'stepping stone' theorists to reinforce their theories. However, spores or seeds of plants might have been carried to the islands by the winds; ocean currents could have floated rafts of vegetation from the mainland; migratory birds could have transported the spores and seeds in their feathers or sticking to their feet; and animal organisms could have arrived on rafts of logs or other debris, carried by the currents. Indeed, it is inherently more likely that the spores or seeds of plants came by these means. Also, the fact that the only land mammals native to the islands are a few species of bats and rats seems to argue *against* the land-bridge theory. There would surely be more species if it had ever existed.

Many of the forms of life which reached the islands failed to adapt to the new environment and died. The survivors have evolved through natural selection into the unique forms we can see there today.

'Natural selection,' says the standard Galapagos guide, 'is the process which favours those individuals or groups of organisms which are best suited to their particular environment.' As the colonising population becomes established, variations may develop within the group. Natural selection then ensures that only the fittest will survive, and through this process the population begins to differ from its original ancestors. Competition is part of natural selection. When two or more species compete for the same resources and one of them is better equipped to compete, it may force out the rival species. Other environmental factors also have their effects. For example, specialisation on some foods, the absence of predators and a climate making migration unnecessary have all clearly contributed to the evolution of the flightless cormorant. Further changes may come about when animals and plants break away from the original colonising population and develop separately in an isolated part of the archipelago. Entirely new populations may grow from these which are better suited to the new environment. The classic example of this in animal populations are the finches which Darwin studied.

While their geographical isolation is the most important factor distinguishing the Galapagos from most environments, there are, of course, other equally or more remote archipelagos – the Marquesas in the Pacific and the Seychelles in the Indian Ocean, for example. However, the Galapagos has a unique environmental feature which is of great importance: its climate. The influence of the Humboldt current on early navigation is shown by the experience of the voyagers recorded in previous chapters. This great stream brings its cold waters sweeping up from the Antarctic. Until near the equator it follows the western coast of the continent, but then swings westward across the Pacific to pass through the Galapagos. From June to December the Humboldt current brings a long cool season to the islands. During this season, there is less than 20 millimetres average rainfall per month, but a fine mist, the garua, forms, particularly on high ground, providing enough moisture to encourage lush vegetation at these levels. The cold current is displaced from December to May by a warmer current coming down from north to south, and known as El Niño (the Child) because it appears normally at Christmas time. The Niño current brings higher sea and air temperatures, and much higher precipitation, which can vary from 25–150 millimetres per month from year to year with large local variations.

On rare occasions the Niño current extends much further south and the resultant changes of temperature have disastrous ecological effects on the vast concentrations of fish and sea birds which flourish in the cold waters off the coast of Peru. The fish population is decimated, the sea birds die from lack of sustenance, and the fish-canning and guano industries suffer. In these 'Niño years' other unusual conditions – winds, storms and cloudbursts – disrupt the Galapagos climate itself, adding a variable factor to the peculiarity of the environment.

In normal years the climate of the Galapagos is remarkably temperate. The cold waters coming up from the Antarctic make this archipelago the coolest place anywhere on the equator. The climatic conditions and the resultant vegetation vary enormously from island to island and, for the bigger ones, even within each island. The surface of the land is one factor behind these variations. Where the lava is of recent origin little or nothing can grow. Where it is old and weathered through time, pockets of soil have been created from eroded rocks and volcanic ash, and vegetable growth can develop. However, it is the airstream and ocean currents, particularly the Humboldt, which have the greatest influence on the development of plant life, determining the amount, form and timing of the rain and garua.

On one of the largest islands, Santa Cruz, there are no less than seven vegetative zones between sea level and the 900-metre uplands. First, there is a narrow shore zone followed by an arid belt reaching to about 150 metres above sea level, and characterised by tree cactus, palo santo and prickly pear. Then comes a more humid transitional zone with slightly bigger trees growing as best they can in the shallow soil. This is succeeded, as the temperature falls and the humidity rises, by a dense and shady moist zone, sometimes called cloud forest. Here everything grows thickly in a lush jungle, including the scalesia tree, related to the sunflower and the daisy. The fifth zone is called the brown zone and it is followed by the miconia belt at about 400 metres. Here the miconia robinsonia bush, which is found nowhere else in the world, grows in dense stands from 1.8 to 3 metres high. The highest zone is the pampas or moorland area of bracken and ferns, with occasional patches of reindeer lichen. All this variety occurs virtually on the equator and within a distance of a few lateral kilometres.

No two islands are alike and on any one, as on Santa Cruz, conditions can change astonishingly. Sometimes even the moist jungle area can be hit by drought since the volcanic soil will not retain water and dries up unless constantly replenished. Low islands receive less moisture than high islands. The prevailing wind is from the south-east and so on high islands the southern slopes are wetter and the northern slopes tend to be arid.

Having examined the islands in some detail, it may be helpful at this point to identify each of them as clearly as possible. The first map showing the islands separately were made by an English buccaneer, William Ambrose Cowley, who chose to name them after the establishment notables of his time. Many of his names have stuck from that day to this. Subsequently the British Navy, the United States Navy, and the Spanish Navy have each had a try at imposing their own names. When Ecuador claimed sovereignty over the archipelago in 1832 it made some changes of its own. Nobody would challenge Ecuador's right to name its islands however it pleases, but unfortunately it has been no more consistent about this than the various explorers and naval officers who came before. In 1892, by way of commemorating the 400th anniversary of Columbus's first voyage, the National Assembly of Ecuador decided to rename the archipelago after him, and to give each of the islands an official name in Spanish, but they did not adopt the Spanish names already in use.

The result of all this naming and renaming is a great deal of confusion. The title Archipelago de Colón (the form of Columbus's name which is normally used in Spanish) has never replaced that of Galapagos in everyday usage, and many of the islands have two or more names in current use, not to mention those which have been superseded. For example, the Duke of Norfolk's Island (as the pirates had it) was changed to Indefatigable by the Royal Navy, to Porter Island after the Captain of the USS *Essex*, then to Valdez, Chavez, San Clemente and finally to Santa Cruz by the Ecuadorian authorities. The original English names used in this book and some of their old and new alternatives are as follows:

ORIGINAL ENGLISH	SPANISH/ENGLISH	OFFICIAL ECUADORIAN
Abingdon	—	Pinta
Albemarle	Santa Isabela	Isabela
Barrington	—	Santa Fé
Bindloe	Diablo	Marchena
Brattle	—	Tortuga
Charles	Floreana	Santa Maria
Chatham	Santa Maria de la Aguada	San Cristóbal
Cowley	—	Cowley
Culpepper	—	Darwin
Duncan	Tabaco	Pinzón
Hood	—	Española
Duke of Norfolk's Island	Indefatigable	Santa Cruz
James	Santiago	San Salvador
Jervis	—	Rabida
Narborough	—	Fernandina
Seymour	—	Baltra
Tower	Salud	Genovesa
Wenman	—	Wolf

In this book, I have followed the general practice of using the island names which were in normal contemporary use. This means that the official Ecuadorian names are used only in the later chapters. For the sake of clarity (so far as it can be achieved in this tricky field), the original English names have been added in parentheses after the Ecuadorian (or Spanish) names.

4

The Buccaneers

T HE THRUST OF SPANISH expansion into the Pacific and beyond
continued through most of the sixteenth century and reached
its apogee in 1567 with Alvaro de Mendaña's first crossing of the
Pacific. Spanish power dominated Europe and the sea routes to
America, as well as the whole of Central and South America.
However, eventually seamen from the smaller states of Northern
Europe began to follow in the wake of Spanish and Portuguese
navigators and adventurers. Sir Francis Drake made his first voyage
to the east coast of South America as a captain under his uncle, John
Hawkins, in the very year of Mendaña's voyage. In a second voyage
in 1577 Drake passed the Straits of Magellan, reconnoitred the west
coast, and on February 13th, 1578 appeared at Callao, the port of
Lima. Soon afterwards Drake and his men captured the Spanish
treasure ship, *Nuestra Señora de la Immaculada Concepción*, known
as Cacafuego by the Spanish sailors, and 'found in her some fruite
… a certain quantitie of jewels and precious stones, 13 chests of
ryals of plate, 80 pound weight in gold, 26 tunne of uncoyned silver
… valued in all about 360,000 pezos.' This booty they divided up on
the Isla de la Plata (Silver Island) where, tradition still maintains,
some of it was buried. This is the origin of legends of 'pieces of
eight' which much later drew pirates from the Caribbean into the
Pacific hoping to emulate Drake's success. To this day treasure

hunters dig on La Plata hoping to find the Spanish gold or silver which Drake is supposed unaccountably to have left behind.

Drake may not have believed in the existence of the Galapagos, and he certainly paid them no attention. Sir Richard Hawkins, the son of John Hawkins, following in Drake's course in 1593, dismissed them as 'a heape of islands the Spaniards call Islas de los Galapagos; they are desert and bear no fruite'. Hawkins' successors must have felt likewise because there are no records of any other British ships touching the islands for almost a century after his voyage.

The next known visit was by the Dutch explorer, Jacob Herenite Clerk, who led a fleet of eleven ships with two hundred and ninety-four cannon and over one thousand six hundred armed men and besieged Lima for five months in 1624. Eventually Clerk was forced to withdraw to the Galapagos, and he later died off Callao before his expedition returned to Holland.

The status of these Protestant seamen from Northern Europe, in what the Spanish regarded as a private lake, was in hot dispute. In 1493 the Spanish Pope Alexander VI granted to the Spanish crown all the territories discovered or to be discovered west of a line drawn from one Pole to the other and passing 370 leagues (1,800 kilometres) to the west of the Cape Verde Islands. The papacy, in an assertion of its temporal power and dynastic preference, made a present of half a world to a Christian king with the sole condition that the king and his subjects should make it their first business and priority to convert the peoples of the New World to Christianity. This was accepted throughout the Catholic world, but national rivalry, the Reformation and the growth of Protestantism meant that there were countries and peoples which did not accept Spain's monopoly. In North America, where Spanish power was relatively weak, the British, Dutch and French could explore, settle and trade with relative freedom. The only obstacles there were the elements, the hardships of the wilderness and the resistance of the indigenous peoples. South of the Gulf of Mexico, there was the organised power of the leading European nation to contend with, and Spain backed up its legal claim and physical occupation of strategic points by banning all foreign ships from trading with its colonies. This added injury to insult and led to a state of sporadic conflict in the New World even when there was peace in Europe. It came to be accepted that there was 'no peace beyond the line', referring to the line laid down by Alexander VI.

King Francis I of France summed up the feelings of the European powers thus excluded by asking to see 'that clause in Adam's will which allowed the Kings of Castille and Portugal to divide the Earth between them'. It was not to be expected that the governments of the debarred nations would be greatly concerned to suppress piracy against Spanish and Portuguese property in time of peace. In wartime the pirates and their ships rapidly became proper naval forces, and they were, in fact, national assets from that point of view. Some were authorised by their own governments as privateers, that is, independently financed men-of-war. Others, including Drake, were alternately buccaneers in the true sense and admirals or captains of their monarch's ships. The Spanish authorities, naturally enough, tended to regard them all as pirates outside the law, fit only to be hanged or turned over to the Inquisition. Even today El Draque (Drake) is spoken of in South America as well as in Spain as an ogre, and his name is used to frighten children into good behaviour. No one else is prepared to share the British view of him as a naval commander of genius and staunch defender of the Protestant religion.

It must be remembered that when English buccaneers first arrived in the Pacific, England was in open conflict with Spain and usually at war. Through the later decades of the sixteenth century Philip II devoted increasingly vigorous military efforts to overthrowing the Protestant Queen Elizabeth I, whom he had once proposed to marry. Spain objected to British pinpricks in the Americas, while at the same time threatening to invade England itself, to depose Elizabeth and to suppress the Protestant religion.

The great Spanish Armada of 1588 was the first of several invasion attempts. Three more Armadas were launched against England before the end of Elizabeth's reign, and she also had to survive a succession of assassination attempts inspired from abroad. However, after Philip's death in 1598 and Elizabeth's in 1603, the long war between Spain and England petered out. The Stuart kings were generally accepted by Christian Europe as legitimate, and usually saw more advantage in appeasing the Spanish crown than opposing it.

Official encouragement or tolerance may have lapsed after the turn of the century, but the buccaneers flourished in the Caribbean, particularly during the Civil War in England (1642–52) and the years immediately afterwards. The pickings there were rich enough to occupy them, and so it was not until the sacking of Panama by Henry Morgan in 1671 that a number of them were tempted to move into the Pacific again. This first group, following Morgan's example and led by men such as John Coxon and Bartholomew Sharp, made the hazardous crossing of the isthmus of Panama overland and began their operations at sea in captured ships.

For a century and a half the Aztecs, the Incas and other native populations of Panama and Peru had cowered under Spanish depredations; now it was the Spaniards' turn to face the attacks, actual or threatened, of the buccaneers. The Spanish authorities knew that the imaginations of these ruthless freebooters had been diverted from the increasingly protected sea routes in the Caribbean (the Spanish Main) to the South Seas, and were filled with alarm. As one of the buccaneers who was to become famous through his adventures, William Dampier, reported:

> Before my going to the South Seas, I being then on board a privateer off Portobel, we took a packet from Carthagena. We opened a great many of the merchants' letters, several of which informed their correspondents of a certain prophecy that went about Spain that year, the tenor of which was that the English

privateers in the West Indies would that year open a door into the South Seas.

In 1675 the Viceroy of Peru heard a rumour that pirate ships had been seen off Chile and sent one of his own vessels to investigate. The rumour proved groundless but the Spanish continued in a nervous state until at last, in 1680, the first group arrived. Loot was their only object, as Captain Bartholomew Sharp tells us with engaging candour: 'Twas gold was the bait that tempted a pack of us Merry Boys, near three hundred in number, being all soldiers of fortune.' He and the other 'Merry Boys' were by no means all British: French and Dutch pirates acted jointly with the British at various times against Spanish and Portuguese property ashore and afloat. Ironically, British trade in its turn suffered great losses at the hands of Spanish privateers. However, this influx into the Pacific seems to have been led by the British or, more accurately, by men from the West Country of England. Certainly it was from these men that the first accurate information about the Galapagos was obtained.

Bart Sharp arrived there in a captured vessel in 1680, but failed to land because of the usual difficulties that all sailing vessels encountered with the winds and currents of Las Encantadas. Next to arrive was a motley group of seventy under the leadership of John Cook (not to be confused with the more famous navigator, Captain James Cook). This mixed bunch of desperadoes, which included Dampier, Lionel Wafer, Ambrose Cowley and Edward Davis, had set out in August 1683 from the newly-founded British colony of Maryland. They sailed from Chesapeake in the eighteen-gun sloop, *Revenge*, which they soon decided was too small for their ambitious purpose of attacking armed and escorted Spanish treasure ships on the west coast of South America between Lima and Panama. They therefore first made their way across the Atlantic via the Cape Verde Islands to the coast of Guinea near the River Sirileone (Sierra Leone). They knew that they would find large and well-equipped ships in that area, since it was the centre of the slave trade in which all maritime countries were then heavily and profitably engaged, and indeed they fell in with a large Danish slaver of forty guns which Captain John Cook and his men managed to board and overpower. 'We found she was very fit for a long voyage, for she was well stored with good brandy, water, provisions and other necessaries.'

The records and journals which were kept by members of Cook's crew (who were some of the most literate of pirates as we shall see) are very reticent about this exploit. It was an act of flagrant piracy punishable by death and completely contrary to the laws of all civilized states. Denmark was a friendly country, and the ship and her crew engaged in what was then regarded as a legitimate trade. So it is not surprising that the perpetrators of the crime burnt their old vessel and failed to explain what became of the Danish crew. Nor do they say what fate befell the sixty black girls they found on the Danish ship, although there is a jocular clue in the fact that they promptly renamed their ship the *Batchelor's Delight*. She was now to become perhaps the most famous, and certainly the most written about, buccaneering ship of her time.

In their new ship and supplied with all they could wish in the way of creature comforts, the 'Merry Boys' made their way back across the Atlantic and southward towards the Magellan Straits. Dampier, who was sailing master, thought it too risky to attempt the route through the Straits without charts and with a crew of dubious worth, so they decided to sail round Cape Horn. Ambrose Cowley's *Voyage Round the World* gives revealing sidelights on the pirates' preoccupations:

> Then haling away south west we came abreast of Cape Horn the 14th day of February, 1684, when we chusing of Valentines and discoursing of the intrigues of women, there arose a prodigious storm which did continue till the last day of the month, driving us into the latitude of 60 degrees and 30 minutes south, which is

further than ever any ship hath sailed before south, so that we concluded the discoursing of women at sea was very unlucky and occasioned the storm...

Towards the beginning of the month of March, the wind coming up at south, we were soon carried into warm weather again; for the weather in the lat. of 60 deg. was so extream cold that we could bear drinking three quarts of Brandy in twenty-four hours each Man and he not at all the worse for it, provided it were burnt.

The *Batchelor's Delight* fought her way round the Horn eventually, despite ferocious storms, and fell in with another pirate ship, the *Nicholas*, commanded by Captain Eaton. Together they made for the safe haven of Juan Fernandez Islands (off the coast of Chile) to recuperate for a few weeks and, if possible, restock after the rigours of the voyage. By 1684 the defence of the Spanish colonies was much better organised than it had been in the days of Drake and Hawkins, so that it was unwise for interlopers to sail inshore and give notice of their presence. Islands such as Juan Fernandez, Lobos de la Mar (off northern Peru) and the Galapagos were among the relatively few hide-outs which the buccaneers could use while waiting for good prizes and preparing their attacks. From Juan Fernandez they sailed cautiously northwards to Lobos where they careened their ships and waited for a week or so longer until three Spanish ships appeared. These were captured without great difficulty but, infuriatingly for the gold-hungry pirates, the cargoes were found to consist of timber, flour and 'eight tons of quince marmalade'. Later they learned to their disgust that the largest of these captured ships had apparently sailed from Lima carrying 800,000 pieces of eight but had landed this great treasure again at Guanchaco as soon as she heard reports of the pirates' presence nearby.

Realising that they had lost the element of surprise and might face Spanish reprisals at any time, they decided to retire to the

Galapagos with their three prizes. The passage was described by Edward Davis:

> Wee lay at Lobos above eight and forty houres, and knowing that we had more than an hundren prisoners on board, not knowing where to get water nor where to find a place for making a Magazene for flower, wee sailed away to the westward to see if we could find those Islands called the Galipoloes, which made the Spaniards laugh telling us that they were inchanted islands and that there was never any but one Capitaino Porialto that had ever seene them, but could not come near them to anchor there, and that they were but shadowes and noe reall islands.

However, the buccaneers' decision was proved right. The islands were real and this visit of the *Batchelor's Delight* was the first occasion on which men ever set foot on most of them. One of those who did so, Ambrose Cowley, found time in this short stay to make the first true chart of the islands and to give them their first names. He explains the naming process in his book:

> . . . Thereupon we stood away to the Westward, to try if we could find those Islands which the Spaniards call Gallappagos or Enchanted Islands, when after three weeks sail we saw land, consisting of many islands, and I being the first that came to an anchor there, did give them all distinct Names.
>
> The first that we saw lay near the lat. of 1 deg. 30 min. South; we having the Wind at South and being on the North side thereof, that we could not sail to get to it, to discover what was upon it. This Island maketh high Land, the which I called King Charles' Island: And we had sight of three more which lay to the Northward of this, that next it I called Crossman's Island; the next to that Brattle's; and the third, Sir Anthony Dean's Island. We moreover saw many more to the Westward. . .
>
> Then we came to an Anchor in a very good Harbour, lying

toward the Northernmost end of a fine Island under the Equinoctial Line. Here being great plenty of Provisions, as Fish, Sea and Land Tortoises, some of which weighed at least 200 Pound weight, which are excellent good Food. Here are also abundance of Fowls, viz. Flemingoes and Turtle Doves; the latter whereof were so tame, that they would often alight upon our Hats and Arms, so as that we could take them alive, they not fearing Man, until such time as some of our Company did fire at them, whereby they were rendered more shy. This Island I called the Duke of York's Island: there lying to the Eastward of that (a fine round Island) which I called the Duke of Norfolk's Island. And to the Westward of the Duke of York's Island, lieth another curious Island, which I called the Duke of Albemarle's, in which is a commodious Bay or Harbour, where you may ride Landlock'd: And before the said Bay lieth another Island, the which I called Sir John Narborough's: And between York and Albemarle's Island lieth a small one, which my fance led me to call Cowley's enchanted Island; for we having had a sight of it upon several points of the Compass, it appear'd always in as many different Forms, sometimes like a ruined Fortification; upon another Point, like a great City etc. This Bay or Harbour in the Duke of York's Island I called Albany Bay; and another Place York Road. Here is excellent good, sweet Water, Wood, etc, and a rich Mineral Ore. From thence we sailed to the Northward, where we saw three more fine Islands (Abingdon, Wenman, Culpepper). All of them that we were at were very plentifully stored with the aforesaid Provisions, as Tortoises, Fowls, Fish and Alguanoes, large and good, but we could find no good Water on any of all these places, save on that of the Duke of York's Island. But at the north end of Albemarle Island there were thick, green Leaves of a thick substance which we chewed to quench our thirst; and there were abundance of Fowls on this Island which could not live without Water, tho we could not find it.

> After that we had laid up, and put on shoar at Albany Bay and other Places, 1500 Bags of Flower, with Sweetmeats, etc., we sailed to the Northward again to try a second time amongst the Islands, if we could find any fresh Water, if ever we should have occasion to touch hereafter amongst them, but it happened so that we fell in with such a very strong current that when we would have sailed back again to the Duke of York's Island to have watered our Ship, we could not stem it. This made us steal away N.N.E. and the first Land that we made upon the Main was Cape Trespontas.

In choosing his names, Cowley took the wise course of doing honour not only to the king and other great figures of the time in England, but also to notables nearer at hand whose goodwill might be or had already proved helpful. The first island he saw he patriotically called King Charles' Island. Another which had a fine harbour was named after the Duke of York, but when Charles II died and his brother became James II, Cowley dutifully renamed it King James' Island. The largest island of all he astutely named Albemarle after George Monk, first Duke of Albemarle, the general who had helped restore Charles II to the throne and who had favoured the buccaneers when he visited Jamaica in 1687. Similarly Wenman and Brattle were called after Lord Wainman and Nicholas Brattle of Jamaica, and Bindloe after Colonel Robert Bindloss who was a member of the Jamaica Council and brother-in-law of Henry Morgan.

The *Batchelor's Delight* spent most of this first visit at James' Island. Captain Cook had fallen sick and they had to make a tent for him ashore. Cowley transferred to one of the prize ships and could thus see more of the islands. After a fortnight they had restocked with fresh tortoise, iguana and turtle meat, and sailed off for the Mexican coast. There Cook finally died of his illness and the crew elected Edward Davis to succeed him. Some sort of rough-and-ready democracy evidently operated among these unruly men, who frequently mutinied and replaced their captains and other officers with new, and presumably more acceptable, ones. Davis was, however, to maintain the command of the *Batchelor's Delight* for the rest of her long voyage.

She returned to Galapagos in 1685 to restock from the reserves of flour cached there during the first visit. Much of it had been broken into by the turtle doves, but they took away five hundred sacks, replenished with water and careened the ship. After sacking Guayaquil in 1687, Davis brought the *Batchelor's Delight* back for a third time.

Records of these two further visits are relatively sketchy, but the surgeon of the *Batchelor's Delight*, Lionel Wafer, recorded that the plunder taken at Guayaquil was divided 'by a very ingenious and unobjectionable mode of distribution. The silver was first divided; the other articles were then put up at auction and bid for in pieces of eight, and when all were so disposed of, a second division was made of the silver produced by the sale.' However, Wafer was disillusioned by now: 'We continued rambling about to little purpose, sometimes at sea, sometimes ashore, till having spent much time and visited many places, we were got again to Galapagos from whence we were determined to make the best of our way out of these seas.'

After another difficult passage round the Horn, the *Batchelor's Delight* finally got back to the West Indies in 1688, just in time to take advantage of the free pardon offered by James II to all buccaneers who abandoned piracy in favour of legal and peaceful pursuits.

In fact, the *Batchelor's Delight* had never achieved very much success. She had waited in the Pacific, with many other pirate ships of various nationalities, for more than four years without winning the jackpot: quince jam was not what the 'Merry Boys' had come into the Pacific to find. Despite the stories of our childhood in which pirates more often than not got away with the treasure (if only to bury it on some remote island for others to search for years later), the buccaneers in the Pacific in the last decades of the seventeenth century usually failed to outwit the Spaniards. However, the threat they presented was very real for Spain in a period of turbulence in Europe, for the loss of even one treasure ship at that time could have very dire consequences. If the Spanish armies were not paid, or not adequately equipped or provisioned for their campaigns, the usual cause was the loss of a ship in transit with gold and silver from the Indies.

The threat was made vividly clear in May 1685 when several contingents of both English and French buccaneers, with others amounting to almost one thousand men, were assembled in ten ships in the Bay of Panama, like vultures waiting to fall on their prey. The English were led by Davis in the *Batchelor's Delight* and Swan in the *Cygnet*. The other parties, one of about three hundred men and comprising both English and French, were led by Groguiet and L'Escuyier, and by Rose, Le Picard and Desmarais. Eventually a Spanish fleet of fourteen arrived from Lima and prepared to give battle. Since the buccaneers suspected that the treasure was no longer aboard the Spanish ships, they had no great enthusiasm for a fight. The Dons eventually lost their appetite for battle as well and after two days of inconclusive manœuvring by the two fleets, the Spaniards retreated to the safety of their port. The only casualties among the pirates were one man killed, six wounded and half a rudder shot away.

Afterwards, the French and English fell out in recriminations over this inglorious affair and went their separate ways. With the widening breach between France and England in Europe, co-operation even in pursuit of piracy became impossible. The buccaneers were still active in the Spanish Main a century later, but they were never again as formidable as in Morgan's time.

5

The Literary Pirates

THE MEN WHO EMBARKED on piratical voyages have been called the scum of the earth. Certainly, they were ruthless, greedy, quarrelsome and cruel, but they were also patriotic, resourceful and brave. Like Drake, Hawkins and Raleigh a century earlier, they might finish their lives as national heroes, as criminals on the gallows, or as traitors on the block, depending on chance and the political climate. Few of the buccaneers had very much formal education, but they were usually men of outstanding ability in one field or another, with enquiring minds and keen eyes. These qualities shine out plainly from the journals and other records which many of them wrote about their adventures and finally published when they returned home.

As we have already seen, one pirate, Ambrose Cowley, left us a mass of factual information about the Galapagos. His maps were the most accurate ones available up to the end of the eighteenth century, and were only fully superseded by Captain Robert Fitzroy's charts, produced after his long and painstaking hydrographic work with HMS *Beagle* in the 1830s. The original of Cowley's principal map contains a footnote which neatly sums up the general picture of the archipelago held by mariners of his time:

These islands derive their name from the resort of Tortoises to them in order to lay their eggs; for in Spanish, Gallapagos signifies a Tortoise. The Buccaneers who had frequent occasion for such places sailed thither often (and) found them very convenient retreats. Captain Woodes Rogers who had a very indifferent opinion of Discoveries made by these sort of people, complains that he was deceived by Captain Davis's account of these Islands, and asserts he could not find a drop of fresh water upon any of them, yet succeeding Navigators have found them agreeable to this Description which is indeed the only good one we have.

However, the greatest of all the literary pirates was certainly William Dampier. While Cowley was interested in charting the islands and recording baldly what he found on them, no detail of botany, zoology, hydrography or meteorology was too small to engage Dampier's interest and powers of observation. He was really more of an explorer and a naturalist than a buccaneer at which he was, in fact, remarkably unsuccessful. He made three voyages round the world. The first of these lasted from 1679 to 1691, on which he must have changed ship half a dozen times or more. He was among the first group of English sailors to set foot on the islands in 1684 and he was to return to them twenty-five years later under a slightly more respectable captain, Woodes Rogers, whose 'indifferent opinion' of buccaneers was delivered so crushingly to Ambrose Cowley.

Dampier had a true scientist's curiosity and an impressive determination to observe and record facts as a preliminary to deduction. The new fashion for scientific enquiry had been greatly stimulated by Charles II's foundation of the Royal Society and his real personal interest in many branches of science. Dampier was almost a contemporary of Isaac Newton, and he dedicated his *New Voyage Round the World* to the President of the Royal Society when it was published in 1697. The success of this book, which gave the world the first printed account of the Galapagos islands, brought

Dampier a considerable reputation and a good deal more money than his efforts at buccaneering had done.

Dampier's description of the Galapagos islands as he found them on his first arrival is (in part) as follows:

The Spaniards who first discovered them, and in whose drafts alone they are laid down, report them to be a great number, stretching northwest from the line, as far as five degrees north, but we saw not above fourteen or fifteen. They are some of them seven or eight leagues long, and three or four broad. They are of a good height, most of them flat and even on top; four or five of the easternmost are rocky, barren and hilly, producing neither tree, herb nor grass; but a few dildo trees, except by the sea side. The dildo tree is a green prickly shrub that grows about ten or twelve feet high, without either leaf or fruit. It is as big as a man's leg, from the root to the top, and it is full of sharp prickles, growing in thick rows from top to bottom; this shrub is fit for no use, not so much as to burn. Close by the sea there grows in some places bushes of Burtonwood, which is very good firing. This sort of wood grows in many places in the West Indies... I never saw any in these seas but there. There is water on these barren islands, in ponds and holes among the rocks. Some other of these islands are mostly plain and low, and the land more fertile; producing trees of divers sorts, unknown to us. Some of the westernmost of these islands are nine or ten leagues long and six or seven broad, the mould deep and black. These produce trees of great and tall bodies, especially mammee-trees, which grow here in great groves. In these large islands there are some pretty big rivers, and on many of the lesser islands there are brooks of good water. The Spaniards when they first discovered these islands, found multitudes of guanoes (iguanas) and land turtle or tortoise, and named the Gallipagos islands. I do believe there is no place in the world that is so plentifully stored with these animals. The guanoes here are as fat and large as any that I ever saw; they are so tame that a man may knock down twenty in an hour's time with a club. The land-turtle are here so numerous that 500 or 600 men might subsist on them alone for several months, without any other sort of provision. They are extraordinarily large and fat, and so sweet, that no pullet eats more pleasantly. One of the largest of these creatures will weigh one hundred and fifty to two hundred weight, and some of them are two feet, or two feet six inches over the callapee or belly. I never saw any but at this place, that will weigh above thirty pounds weight...

The air of these islands is temperate enough considering the clime. Here is constantly a fresh sea breeze all day, and cool refreshing winds in the night; therefore the heat is not so violent here, as in most places near the equator. The time of the year for the rains is in November, December and January; then there is oftentimes excessive dark tempestuous weather, mix'd with much thunder and lightning. Sometimes before and after these months there are moderate refreshing showers; but in May, June, July and August, the weather is always very fair.

We staid at one of these islands, which lies under the equator, but one night, because our prizes could not get in to anchor. We refresh'd ourselves very well, both on land and sea turtles, and the next day we sailed thence. The next island of Gallipagos that we came to is but two leagues from this; it is rocky and barren like this; it is about five or six leagues long, and four broad. We anchored in the afternoon at the north side of the island, a quarter of a mile from the shore, in sixteen-fathom water. It is steep all round this island and no anchoring only at this place. Here it is but ordinary riding, for the ground is so steep, that if an anchor starts it never holds again, and the wind is commonly off from the land, except in the night, when the landwind comes more from the west; for there it blows right along the shore, though but faintly. Here is no water but in ponds and holes of the rocks. That which we first anchored at hath water on the north end, falling down in a stream from high steep rocks, upon the sandy bay, where it may be taken up.

As soon as we came to an anchor, we made a tent ashore for Captain Cook, who was sick. Here we found the turtle lying ashore on the sand; this is not customary in the West Indies. We turned them on their backs that they might not get away. The next day more came up; when we found it to be their custom to lie in the sun, we never took care to turn them afterwards, but sent ashore the cook every morning, who killed as many as served for the day. This custom we observed all the time we lay here, feeding sometimes on land turtle, sometimes on sea turtle, there being plenty of either sort... The sea about these islands is plentifully stored with fish, such as are at Juan Fernandes. They are both large and fat and as plentiful here as at Juan Fernandes; here are particularly abundance of sharks. The north part of this second isle we anchored at lies 28 minutes north of the equator, for I took the height of the sun with an astrolabe. These isles of the Gallipagos have plenty of salt. We stayed here but twelve days, in which time we put ashore 5,000 packs of flour for a reserve if we should have occasion for any before we left these seas.

This has a similar flavour and character to Charles Darwin's account written one hundered and fifty years later. Darwin, however, was the official naturalist on a properly organised voyage backed by the Admiralty and all the resource, if not all the resources, of the Royal Navy. On his first visit to the islands, Dampier was an entirely unofficial naturalist on an expedition whose only common purpose was piracy. It is a minor miracle that his notes even survived the hurly-burly of a twelve-year Odyssey in the roughest of conditions. He tells us that 'I took care to provide myself with a large joint of bamboo which I stopped at both ends, closing it with wax so as to keep out any water. In this I preserved my journal and other writings from being wet, though I was often forced to swim.' Dampier's achievement in actually maintaining a detailed record of his observations can stand comparison even with Darwin's.

However, the greatest impact of Dampier's *New Voyage Round the World* may be that it set a fashion for travel literature which has flourished ever since. He was one of the few early visitors to the Galapagos who seemed to derive any great enjoyment from what he found there. Perhaps this was because he apparently arrived at a time when exceptionally heavy rain had produced good supplies of fresh water in the springs. It seems likely that the well-watered island he describes was Santa Cruz. Almost everyone else who has visited the Galapagos found the lack of water a major nuisance if not a hazard to life, but Dampier describes an agreeable environment full of vegetation, trees, wild life and even 'some pretty big rivers'.

Repenting his piratical past, Dampier became respectable and was put in command of a ship which was despatched by the Admiralty to continue the exploration of Australasia. Here his name is commemorated in various places – Dampier Island and Dampier Strait, for example – but the voyage was not a great success, and he seems to have preferred thereafter to avoid the burdens of command. Certainly he was content to embark on his final voyage round the world as pilot and navigator to an expedition led by Captain Woodes Rogers in 1708 to 1711, during the War of the Spanish Succession. This was a privateering voyage, financed by a group of Bristol merchants for their own profit, but Woodes Rogers treated it also as a naval expedition, intended to make Britain's presence felt by enemy forces in the South Seas. He was given a commission from the Lord High Admiral to wage war on the Spanish, and on the French with whom Britain was by then officially at war. Rogers' 'fleet' consisted of the *Duke*, 320 tons and thirty guns, and the *Duchess*, 260 tons and twenty-six. Each had a crew of one hundred sailors of mixed ability and nationality, but the ships were well-equipped and supplied for a long voyage. Rogers regarded himself as the commander of a disciplined force, although he records in his book *A Cruising Voyage Round the World* that, by decision of the owners, the ultimate authority over the expedition was vested in a council of officers, which included Dampier and Doctor Thomas Dover. Dover held the positions of Second Captain and Captain of the Marines, and was also one of the financiers of the enterprise, but his fame depended mostly on his invention, or rather concoction, of Dover Powders, which for many years were the most widely-used specific for the treatment of dysentery.

When the *Duke* and *Duchess* had fought their way round the Horn, they made at once for Juan Fernandez and, after two weeks' respite, Woodes Rogers sailed northwards towards Guayaquil, the main coastal town of modern Ecuador. This was a favourite target for buccaneers and privateers alike, since Lima, the seat of the Spanish Viceroy, was too well defended to be readily susceptible to attack. By this time the English force had learnt that their presence in the Pacific was known to the Spanish authorities. They had captured a prize containing a letter of warning sent by the Viceroy to the Corregidor of Guayaquil and other local authorities to the effect that an English squadron of seven ships (under, it was alleged, a certain Captain Dampier) had sailed from England for the South Seas. Surprise was no longer possible, so Dampier and others in the council of officers were strongly against any attempt on Guayaquil. However, Woodes Rogers eventually had his way, a landing was made and after protracted parleys and negotiations the town was taken by storm. The English managed to extort the fairly small ransom of thirty thousand pieces of eight, over and above the plunder they had taken, as the price for not burning down the town completely.

This episode shows plainly that profit rather than patriotism was the motive uppermost in the minds of all concerned. Rogers records with equanimity that his men even robbed the Guayaquil ladies of the gold jewellery they had concealed under their dresses and takes it as 'proof of our sailors' modesty' that these valuables were found 'by pressing . . . with their hands on the outside of the lady's apparel'. He was proud of the fact that only one of his men was found 'in a Brandy-wine fit' having 'transgressed orders by drinking beyond his bearing'. Pillage and plunder were the very purpose of the expedition, but lechery and drunkenness would not be tolerated, apparently.

Once this operation was complete, the two ships with four prize vessels and a number of prisoners and hostages bore away as fast as they could for the Galapagos, before Spanish or French warships could catch them on the coast. Three days later a 'malignant fever' broke out and spread so rapidly that by the time they sighted the islands on May 16th, 1709, one hundred and forty men were on the sick list. Rogers' journal for the rest of his stay in the Galapagos is a catalogue of deaths caused by this epidemic caught in Guayaquil, apart from constant worry over fresh water. The islands were full of fresh tortoise and iguana meat and the seas full of fish, but very few had fresh water. He never found the spring which Dampier and others had told him the *Batchelor's Delight* had used.

> 19th May. Yesterday in the afternoon the Boat return'd with a melancholy Account, that no Water was to be found. The Prizes we expected would have lain to Windward for us by the Rock about 2 Leagues off Shore; but Mr Hatley in a Bark, and the *Havre de Grace*, turn'd to Windward after our Consort the *Duchess*; so that only the Galleon and the Bark that Mr Selkirk was in staid for us. . . At 5 in the Morning we sent our Boat ashore again to make a further search in this Island for Water. About 10 in the Morning James Danier our Joiner died. We had good Observation, Lat 00°32'S.
>
> 20th May. Yesterday in the Evening our Boat return'd but found no Water, tho they went for 3 or 4 miles up into the country. They tell me the Island is nothing but loose Rocks, like Cynders, very rotten and heavy, and the Earth so parch'd that it will not bear a Man, but break into Holes under his Feet, which

makes me suppose there has been a Vulcano here; tho' there is much shrubby Wood, and some Greens on it, yet there's not the least Sign of Water, nor is it possible, that any can be contain'd on such a Surface. At 12 last Night we lost sight of our Galleon, so that we have only one Bark with us now.

21st May. Yesterday in the Afternoon came down the *Duchess* and the French Prize. The *Duchess's* Bark had caught several Turtle and Fish, and gave us a Part, which was very serviceable to the sick Men, our fresh Provisions that we had got on the main Land being all spent. They were surpriz'd as much as we at the Galleon, and Hatley's Bark being out of sight, thinking before they had been with us. We kept Lights at our Top-mast's Head, and fir'd Guns all Night, that they might either see or hear how to join us, but to no Purpose.

Capt Courtney being not yet quite recover'd, I went on board the *Duchess*, and agreed with him and his officers, to stay here with the *Havre de Grace* and Bark, whilst I went in Quest of the missing prizes. At 6 in the morning we parted, and stood on a Wind to the Eastward, judging they lost us that way. Here are very strange Currents amongst these Islands, and commonly run to Leeward, except on the Full Moon I observed it ran very strong to Windward; I believe 'tis the same at change.

22nd May. Yesterday at 3 in the Afternoon we met with the Galleon under the East Island, but heard nothing of Mr Hatley's Bark. At 9 last Night Jacob Scronder a Dutch-man and a very good Sailor, died. We kept on the Wind in the Morning to look for the Weather Island for Mr Hatley, and fir'd a Gun for the Galleon to bear away for the Rendezvous Rock, which she did.

23rd May. Yesterday at 3 in the Afternoon we saw the Weather Island near enough, and no sail about it. We bore away in sight of the Rock, and saw none but our Galleon; we were in another Fright what became of our consort, and the 2 Prizes we left behind; but by 5 we saw 'em come from under the Shore to the Leeward of the Rock. We spoke with 'em in the Evening; we all bewail'd Mr Hatley and were afraid he was lost; We fir'd Guns all Night, and kept Lights out, in hopes he might see or hear us, and resolv'd to leave these unfortunate Islands, after we had viewed two or three more to Leeward. We pity'd our 5 Men in the Bark that is missing, who if in being have a melancholy Life without Water, having no more but for 2 Days, when they parted from us. Some are afraid they run on Rocks, and were lost in the Night, others that the 2 Prisoners and 3 Negroes had murder'd 'em when asleep; but if otherwise, we had no Water, and our Men being still sick, we could stay little longer for them. Last Night died Law. Carney of a malignant Fever. There is hardly a Man in the Ship, who had been ashore at Guiaquil but has felt something of this Distemper, whereas not one of those that were not there have been sick yet. Finding that Punch did preserve my own Health I prescrib'd it freely among such of the Ship's Company as were well, to preserve theirs. Our Surgeons make heavy Complaints for want of sufficient Medicines, with which till now I thought we abounded . . .

24th May. Yesterday at 5 in the Afternoon we ran to the Northward and made another Island . . . and this Morning we sent our boat ashore, to see for the lost Bark, Water, Fish or Turtle. This Day Tho. Hughes, a very good Sailor, died, as did Mr George Underhill, a good Proficient in most parts of the Mathematics and other Learning, tho' not much above 21 years old. He was of a very courteous Temper, and brave, was in the Fight where my Brother was kill'd, and serv'd as Leiutenant in my Company at Guiaquil. About the same time another young Man, call'd John English, died aboard the *Havre de Grace*, and we have many still sick. . .

25th May. Yesterday at 6 in the Evening our Boat return'd from the Island without finding any Water, or seeing the Bark ... Last night Peter Marshal, a good Sailor, died. This morning our Boat with Mr Selkirk's Bark went to another Island to view it ...

26th May. Last night our Boat and Bark return'd, having rounded the Island, found no Water but Plenty of Turtle and Fish. This Morning we join'd the *Duchess*, who had found no Water. About 12 a Clock we compar'd our Stocks of Water, found it absolutely necessary to make the best of our way to the Main for some, then to come off again; and so much the rather, because we expected that 2 French Ships, one of 60, and another of 40 Guns, with some Spanish Men of War, would suddenly be in quest of us.

30th May. Had we supplied ourselves well at Point Arena, we should, no doubt, have had time enough to find the Island S. Maria de l'Aquada, reported to be one of the Gallapagoes, where there is Plenty of good water, Timber, Land and Sea Turtles, and a Safe Road for Ships. . . It's probable there is such an Island, because one Capt. Davis, an Englishman, who was a buckaneering in these Seas, above 20 Years ago, lay some months and recruited here to Content. He says that it had Trees fit for Masts; but these sort of Men, and others I have convers'd with, or whose Books I have read, have given very blind or false Relations of their Navigation, and Actions in those Parts, for supposing the Places too remote to have their Stories disprov'd, they imposed on the Credulous, amongst whom I was one, till now I too plainly see that we cannot find any of their Relations to be relied on. Therefore I shall say no more of these Islands, since by what I saw of 'em, they don't at all answer the Description that those Men have given us.

The tone of his journal shows clearly how much Woodes Rogers disliked the Galapagos and distrusted most of what he had been told about them. Nevertheless, he is drawn into speculation about the origin of the giant tortoises 'because they can't come of themselves and none of that sort are to be found on the Main (land)'. And, despite his blunt approach to life, he is no more immune than others to the fascination of these extraordinary creatures:

the ugliest in Nature, the shell not unlike the top of an old Hackney coach, as black as Jet, and so is the outside skin, but shrivel'd and very rough; the legs and neck are long and about the bigness of a Man's wrist, and they have Club Feet as big as One's Fist, shaped much like those of an Elephant. . . the Head little and visage small like a snake, and look very old and black . . . Two of our men, with Lieut. Stratton and the Trumpeter of the *Duchess*, affirm that they saw vast large ones of this sort about 4 feet high; they mounted two men on the back of one of them who . . . never minded the weight. They suppos'd this could not weigh less than 700 pound.

The *Duke* and *Duchess* left in May and spent another three months cruising inshore to pick up what further prizes they could. They returned in September 1709 for another respite in the Galapagos and to make a final effort to find Hatley and his companions. Then, being once more low in water, they set sail northwards and, while off the coast of southern California, they finally found a rich prize in the shape of one of the Manila treasure ships on passage to Acapulco. With the success of the venture assured, they made for home across the Pacific and Indian Oceans, eventually landing in Scotland in 1711.

For Dampier this was the final voyage in a long and marvellously adventurous life; we have no record of his last years. Woodes Rogers later became Governor of the Bahamas and died there in 1732. Long after the end of his voyage round the world, he learned that Hatley and his crew had managed to reach the mainland after great suffering, and been thrown into prison until the end of the war in 1714. It is said that Hatley, on a later voyage, achieved a permanent place in English folklore by being the sailor who killed the albatross, immortalised by Coleridge in *The Rime of the Ancient Mariner*. One can only hope that his luck changed in the end and that he had a happy old age.

6

Robinson Crusoes

WHEN THE *Duke* and *Duchess* first reached Juan Fernandez Island on February 1st,1709 Captain Woodes Rogers' only concern was to find fresh supplies and water in the hope that they would cure the attacks of scurvy from which his crew were suffering. While preparing to land that evening, they were alarmed to see a light on shore, and came to the conclusion that it was probably on a French man-of-war. If so, they would have a fight on their hands before they could hope for water. Rogers agreed that his second-in-command, Dr Thomas Dover, should land with a small armed party to investigate cautiously while the ships kept clear. After an anxious wait, Dover's party 'returned from the shore and brought an abundance of craw-fish, with a man cloth'd in Goat-Skins who looked wilder than the first owners of them'.

This proved to be Alexander Selkirk, a Scotsman, who had been Master of the *Cinque-Ports* and had been marooned on the island for four years and four months. Selkirk was to be the model for another and even better known castaway, Robinson Crusoe. It emerged that he had been marooned by Captain Stradling, his commander on the *Cinque-Ports*, with whom he had had one of the usual buccaneer's quarrels. Selkirk had been anxious about their ability to get round Cape Horn on their return journey from the Pacific in a ship which was already leaking. He therefore, preferred to be put ashore rather than face the prospect of drowning. Later, sobered no doubt by thinking about the alternative of life as a castaway, he changed his mind, but Stradling refused to take him back. Selkirk was put ashore at Juan Fernandez, which he knew from a previous visit, and although his experience was terrifying he was able to survive it. As it turned out, Stradling and the rest of the crew of the *Cinque-Ports* suffered even more than Selkirk. His fears about the ship's seaworthiness proved right, and she had to be beached on the mainland, where Stradling and his men were forced to surrender to the Spaniards and spent more years in gaol than Selkirk did in the solitude of his desert island.

The choice between being marooned on an uninhabited island on the far side of the world and, as a buccaneer, being caught by the Spanish authorities while England and Spain were in a state of war, was not a happy one. The unlucky Simon Hatley and his crew suffered the same fate when they, too, were forced to take refuge on Spanish-controlled territory five years later. They were treated not only as prisoners of war but also as heretics, and consequently the priests of the Inquisition were obliged to try to convert their prisoners to the true faith by whatever means seemed most likely to be effective. In the case of Hatley and his companions, it was the simple method of hanging them until they were almost dead and then cutting them down to enquire if they had been converted. We do not know whether Captain Stradling and his crew had similar treatment but the risk of it was always real for any seaman, honest or otherwise, who fell into the enemy's hands in those days. For a man of resource and character, the fate of a castaway may have been preferable. As it transpired, Alexander Selkirk had the strength to survive his ordeal.

Woodes Rogers gave a long account of Selkirk's story in his book, which made Selkirk famous on their return.

He had with him his Clothes and Bedding, with a Firelock some Powder, Bullets, and Tobacco, a Hatchet, a Knife, a Kettle, a Bible, some Practical Pieces, and his Mathematical Instruments and Books. He diverted and provided for himself as well as he could; but for the first eight Months had much ado to bear up against Melancholy and the Terror of being left alone in such a desolate place ... At first he never eat anything till Hunger constrain'd him, partly for grief, and partly for want of Bread and Salt; nor did he go to bed till he could watch no longer. The Piemento Wood, which burnt very clear, serv'd him both for Firing and Candle, and refresh'd him with its fragrant Smell ... His way of living and continual exercise of walking and running, clear'd him of all gross Humours, so that he ran with wonderful Swiftness thro the Woods and up the Rocks and Hills, as we perceived when we employed him to catch Goats for us. We had a Bull-dog, which we sent with several of our nimblest runners, to help him in catching Goats; but he distanc'd and tir'd both the Dog and the Men, catch'd the Goats, and brought 'em to us on his Back. He told us that his agility in pursuing a Goat had once like to have cost him his Life; he Pursu'd it with so much Eagerness that he catch'd hold of it on the brink of a Precipice, of which he was not aware, the bushes having hid it from him; so that he fell with the Goat down the said Precipice and was so stunn'd and bruis'd with the Fall, that he narrowly escaped with his Life, and when he came to his Senses, found the Goat dead under him. He lay there about 24 hours, and was scarce able to crawl to his Hutt, which was about a mile distant, or to stir abroad again in ten days.

... After he had conquer'd his Melancholy, he diverted himself sometimes by cutting his Name on the Trees, and the Time of his being left and Continuance there. He was at first much pester'd with Cats and Rats, that had bred in great numbers from some of each species which had got ashore from Ships that put in there to wood and water. The Rats gnaw'd his Feet and Clothes while asleep which oblig'd him to cherish the Cats with his Goats' flesh; by which many of them became so tame, that they would lie about him in hundreds, and soon deliver'd him from the Rats. He likewise tam'd some Kids, and to divert himself would now and then sing and dance with them and his Cats; so that by the Care of Providence and Vigour of his Youth, being now but about 30 years old, he came at last to conquer all the Inconveniences of his Solitude, and to be very easy. When his Clothes wore out, he made himself a Coat and Cap of Goat-Skins, which he stitch'd together with little Thongs of the same, that he cut with his knife. He had no other Needle than a Nail; and when his Knife was wore to the back, he made others as well as he could of some Iron Hoops that were left ashore, which he beat thin and ground upon Stones . . .

At his first coming on board us, he had so much forgot his Language for want of Use that we could scarce understand him, for he seem'd to speak his words by halves. We offer'd him a Dram, but he would not touch it, having drank nothing but Water since his being there, and 'twas some time before he could relish our Victuals.

This Morning we clear'd up Ship, and bent our Sails, and got them ashore to mend and make Tents for our sick men. The Governor, for so we call'd Mr Selkirk, caught us two Goats, which make excellent Broth, mix'd with Turnip Tops and other Greens, for our sick Men, being 21 in all, but not above two that we count dangerous; the *Duchess* has more Men sick, and in a worse condition than ours.

Rogers went on to ponder the fate of other castaways. One sailor was said to have spent no less than five years on Juan Fernandez when shipwrecked there in the early 1680s from one of the ships which sailed with Captain Bart Sharp. Dampier's book tells of a 'Moskito Indian', that is an Indian from the Mosquito Coast of Central America, who had been marooned there by the heartless Captain Watling, and was taken off in 1684 by the *Batchelor's Delight*. Rogers says, a little sententiously:

One may see that Solitude and Retirement from the World is not such an insufferable State of Life as most men imagine, especially when People are fairly call'd or thrown into it unavoidably, as this Man was . . . we may perceive by this Story the Truth of the Maxim, that Necessity is the Mother of Invention, since he found Means to supply his wants in a very natural manner so as to maintain his life, tho' not so conveniently yet as effectually as we are able to do with the help of all our Arts and Society. It may likewise instruct us, how much a plain and temperate way of living conduces to the Health of the Body and the Vigour of the Mind, both (of) which we are apt to destroy by Excess and Plenty ...

Conscious, perhaps, that he is beginning to sound like an eighteenth-century health faddist, Rogers rounds off the story of Alexander Selkirk by saying: 'but I must quit these Reflections which are more proper for a Philosopher and Divine than a Mariner, and return to my own Subject.'

Selkirk, whose qualities as a sailor were already known to Dampier, was taken on as mate by Woodes Rogers and he slowly adjusted himself to the diet and the social life without which he had survived so well for four years. He played a prominent part in the attack on Guayaquil, and took command of one of the prize ships which sailed with the *Duke* and *Duchess* to the Galapagos in May 1709. There his familiarity with conditions on uninhabited islands was particularly valuable, and over and over again he earned his nickname of 'Governor'.

When Selkirk arrived in Scotland in 1711 with Woodes Rogers and Dampier, he became something of a celebrity. Just as Woodes Rogers was fascinated by the story, so the thoughtful and the curious in Britian were intrigued to speculate on how any man could survive on an uninhabited island for months and years on end, let alone how a civilised man could support the loneliness and isolation of such a place. Daniel Defoe may well have read Woodes

Rogers' book *A Cruising Voyage Round the World* published in 1712, and he is also believed to have seen an account written by Selkirk himself. However he heard the story, Defoe realised that this theme had an irresistible public appeal and set his pen and his imagination to work to turn it into the bestseller Robinson Crusoe. He elaborated and invented much of his story and lifted other elements straight out of the first-hand narratives circulated by the buccaneers themselves. Those who have read both the original logs and journals, and the novel, have all noted the liberal way in which Defoe helped himself to and altered the original material to produce an exciting work of fiction set against an exotic background.

The original of Man Friday was almost certainly the Mosquito Indian, whom Dampier knew as William, rescued by the *Batchelor's Delight*. Another Mosquito, who was already aboard the *Batchelor's Delight*, was the first to greet William and did so by falling full length on the ground in front of his compatriot before rising to embrace him. In Robinson Crusoe Defoe used this form of courtesy for another purpose, when Man Friday is made to prostrate himself on first meeting Crusoe. Europeans of that time took it as a matter of course that the 'savages' they found outside their own continent would become the servants, if not the slaves, of Christians. (Christians were equally likely to be enslaved, or endure a worse fate, if they were captured by Muslims.) Therefore Defoe faithfully reflected the general opinion of his contemporaries when he showed Man Friday unquestioningly accepting, indeed welcoming, the superiority of his master.

If it were not for Defoe's book, the name Alexander Selkirk would mean nothing to us now. There must have been many other castaways whose stories have been lost because their experiences never caught the attention of a writer. Certainly neither Selkirk nor any practical man would have dreamed of leaving his ship for a nearly waterless Galapagos island. Despite this, in due course Charles' Island gained a Robinson Crusoe of its own.

Patrick Watkins was an Irishman who arrived about the beginning of the nineteenth century on an English ship. His story comes to us through the journal published by Captain David Porter, an outstanding officer of the newly-formed United States Navy, who had an exciting and important sojourn in the archipelago during the Anglo-American War of 1812. Porter tells us that Patrick Watkins built himself a crude hut and managed to grow crops of potatoes and other vegetables, which he exchanged for rum or sold for cash to passing ships, mainly whalers.

The appearance of this man, from the accounts I have received of him, was the most dreadful that can be imagined; ragged clothes, scarce sufficient to cover his nakedness, and covered with vermin; his red hair and beard matted, his skin much burnt from constant exposure to the sun, and so wild and savage in his manner and appearance that he struck everyone with horror. For several years this wretched being lived by himself on this desolate spot, without any apparent desire than that of procuring rum in sufficient quantities to keep himself intoxicated, and, at such times, after an absence from his hut of several days, he would be found in a state of perfect insensibility, rolling among the rocks of the mountains. He appeared to be reduced to the lowest grade of which human nature is capable, and seemed to have no desire beyond the tortoises and other animals of the island, except that of getting drunk. But this man, wretched and miserable as he may have appeared, was neither destitute of ambition, nor incapable of undertaking an enterprise that would have apalled the heart of any other man; nor was he devoid of the talent of rousing others to second his hardihood.

Tiring eventually of his island, and perhaps of this degraded life, Patrick somehow got hold of a musket. With it, he abducted a negro sailor sent ashore from an American ship, and announced that the negro would henceforth be his slave. The victim of the hijack found a chance to overpower the Irishman, tied his hands and delivered him helpless to an English smuggling ship which was also in the Charles' Island anchorage at the time. The Captain of this ship ordered Patrick to be whipped on board both his own and the American vessel, and he was afterwards taken ashore again in handcuffs and compelled to give up not only his musket but also the few dollars he had hidden away. This harsh punishment does not seem to have improved Patrick's character. He contrived to escape from his captors and elude them until they finally sailed, when he

ventured from his hiding place and, by means of an old file which he drove into a tree, freed himself from his handcuffs . . .

He now meditated a severe revenge, but concealed his intentions. Vessels continued to touch there, and Patrick, as usual, to furnish them with vegetables; but from time to time he was enabled, by administering potent draughts of his darling liquor to some of the men of the crews, and getting them so drunk that they were rendered insensible, to conceal them until the ship had sailed; when, finding themselves entirely dependent on him, they willingly enlisted under his banners, became his slaves, and he the most absolute of tyrants. By this means he had augmented the number to five, including himself, and every means was used by him to procure arms for them, but without effect. It is supposed that his object was to have surprised some vessel, massacred her crew, and taken her off. While Patrick was meditating his plans, two ships, an American and an English vessel, touched there and applied to Patrick for vegetables. He promised them the greatest abundance, provided they would send their boats to his landing.

The sequel was, of course, that Patrick stole one of the boats and embarked in it with his gang of subjects, supposedly in search of an easier life on the Marquesas Islands, some 5,000 kilometres away across the Pacific. Another ship arriving soon afterwards found in Patrick's deserted hut, the following remarkable letter:

Sir,
I have made repeated applications to captains of vessels to sell me a boat, or to take me from this place, but in every instance met with a refusal. An opportunity presented itself to possess myself of one, and I took advantage of it. I have been a long time endeavouring, by hard labour and suffering, to accumulate wherewithal to make myself comfortable; but at different times have been robbed and maltreated, and in a late instance by captain Paddock, whose conduct in punishing me and robbing me of about five hundred dollars, in cash and other articles, neither agrees with the principles he professes, nor is it such as his sleek coat would lead one to expect.

On the 29 March 1809, I sail from the enchanted island in the *Black Prince*, bound to the Marquesas.

Do not kill the old hen; she is now sitting and will soon have chicks.
Signed
Fatherless Oberlus

In fact, however, the impressively named ship's boat, the *Black Prince* eventually arrived at Guayaquil after a rather shorter journey in the opposite direction. Presumably the reference to the Marquesas was simply to send any pursuers off the wrong way. What is harder to explain is the fact that Patrick was alone when he reached Guayaquil. Captain Porter suggests that he murdered the other men when water supplies began to run out. Other historians have speculated on whether they might have come to an even more gruesome end if food grew short. It does not seem likely that only an Irish alcoholic survived the tortures of thirst and that the others all died of it, but we shall never know. The only other information that Porter gave was that this strange Robinson Crusoe, rather than trying to return home or make himself a life on the mainland of South America, soon wanted to return to the Galapagos. He managed to persuade 'a tawny damsel' in Paita (Peru) to accompany him back to his island in the hope that they might between them establish a permanent population there. This dubious proposal was, however, frustrated when the Peruvian police, suspecting that Pat wanted to steal a boat there, threw him into gaol in Paita. There, the first resident of the Galapagos disappeared from view.

Patrick Watkins, as Porter quickly saw, must have been a man of unusual determination and resource to have survived all the hardships and miseries. In addition, he would not have written the letter quoted above, or signed himself by the extraordinary name of 'Fatherless Oberlus', if he had really been a degraded and scarcely human creature whose only conscious thought was for rum. It is the letter of an educated man, adding another element of mystery to a strange history.

7

The Whale and the Tortoise

FOR THE FIRST TWO-AND-A-HALF centuries of its known history, the governments and people of substance in the Old and New Worlds knew nothing of, or found nothing worthy of notice in, this remote and arid archipelago. However, the eighteenth century was the 'age of enlightenment', and scientific enquiry in the interests of new knowledge was being promoted all over Europe. The Bourbon Kings of Spain, Carlos III and Carlos IV, were accordingly persuaded to send expeditions into the Pacific to undertake general exploration and research, as well as for specific reasons of policy.

Captain Alonso Torres y Guerra of the Spanish Navy reached the Galapagos at the end of an expedition seeking the Northwest Passage. He found little to detain him, produced a map in the record time of four days – which accounted, no doubt, for its deficiencies – and left for home as quickly as he could. A more significant expedition arrived in 1790, led by a Spanish naval officer of Sicilian origin, Alejandro Malaspina. He brought with him a group of experts, including a botanist, a mineralogist and a geographer and they are recorded to have made highly important scientific investigations in the islands. Unfortunately Malaspina fell under political suspicion in Spain, and on his return in 1794 he was immediately thrown into prison in the Castle of San Antonio at La Coruña. The work of his expedition was therefore not published until a century later, and even then some of the findings on the Galapagos were probably left to lie in the archives.

Conditions on the mainland had changed considerably with the decline of Spain's international power. Although the mother country still tried to maintain a total monopoly of trade with her colonies, the colonists themselves were keenly interested in obtaining the manufactured goods which Britain and other European countries could supply. Thus foreign ships trading in these goods were less feared on the west coast of South America, and could normally expect a fairly friendly welcome. Smuggling offered a less risky, and almost equally attractive way of making money, and all concerned preferred it to the very dangerous business of piracy. The smugglers who replaced the buccaneers sometimes found it convenient to use the Galapagos as a safe place to careen and refit their ships, and stock up with fresh tortoise meat. Water was still hard to find, but the supply of giant tortoises was great enough to support smuggling and other vessels indefinitely.

The Galapagos still attracted only small numbers of visiting ships, but this situation was changed sharply as a powerful commercial motive came into play. It is summed up in one startlingly modern word: oil! The impetus of the Industrial Revolution in Europe, particularly in England, was creating a constantly growing demand for oil. At that time, this was supplied not by vegetable or mineral oils, but by the sperm whale. The whaling business in northern waters had been highly important, both commercially and industrially, but by the end of the century the whale catches there were starting to decline due to over-hunting and the whaling industry needed to look further afield for its future.

Some indications of the existence of large numbers of whales in the South Pacific had filtered back to Europe from the stories of the buccaneers. Now more came through Captain James Cook of the Royal Navy. Consequently, the leading British whaling company, Enderby & Sons, began to look for ways to exploit the whale stocks in the Pacific. In 1790 they asked the British Government for help in this and, in particular, for some means of proving to the Spanish colonial authorities that Britain had recently made a treaty with Spain enabling ships in distress in the South Seas to use Spanish ports because 'we have not been able to persuade more than two of our Captains to go round Cape Horn as they are fearful if they meet with any accident or sickly crews, and are in want of water or go into any Spanish port, they will be made slaves for life'.

In 1792 the Royal Navy lent Enderby & Sons the services of Captain James Colnett, and sold them a vessel, HMS *Rattler*, to conduct studies of the practicalities of developing whaling in the South Seas. Colnett already had considerable knowledge of the Pacific, and had made visits of exploration to New Zealand, the New Hebrides, Java and the Sandwich Islands. Although the Napoleonic wars were about to begin, and the war of American Independence was not long past, the Royal Navy had managed to become well-practised in this kind of multipurpose voyage, fulfilling strategic, scientific and commercial purposes at the same time. Colnett's voyage had a defined commercial and mercantile purpose, but it also provided scientific information and other useful data to be noted at the Admiralty for use in any future hostilities in the area. His journal recorded a mass of geographical, zoological and botanical detail as the following extracts concerning the Galapagos show.

> The various kinds of sea-birds which I had seen on the coast of Peru, we found here, but not in equal abundance. There were also flamingoes, sea-pies, plovers and sand-larks. The latter were of the same kind as those of New Zealand. No quadruped was seen on this island, and the greatest part of its inhabitants appeared to be of the reptile kind, as land tortoises, lizards, and spiders. We also saw dead snakes, which probably perished in the dry season. There were, besides, several species of insects, as ants, moths, and the common flies in great numbers; as well as grass-hoppers and crickets.

On the shore were sea guanas and turtle; the latter were of that kind which bears a variegated shell. The guanas are small and of a sooty black, which, if possible, heightens their native ugliness. Indeed, so disgusting is their appearance, that no one on board could be prevailed on to take them as food.

We saw but few seals on the beach, either of the hairy or furry species. This circumstance, however, might be occasioned by its not being the season for whelping... Dampier mentions that there is plenty of salt to be obtained here at this season, but I could not find any ... The rocks are covered with crabs and there are also a few small wilks and winkles. A large quantity of dead shells, of various kinds were washed upon the beach, all of which were familiar to me; among the rest were the shells of large crayfish, but we never caught any of them alive. On several parts of the shore there was driftwood of a larger size than any of the trees that grow on the island; also bamboos and wild sugar canes, with a few small cocoa nuts at full growth though not larger than a pigeon's egg. We observed also some burnt wood, but that might have drifted from the continent, been thrown overboard from a ship, or fired by lightning on the spot. As I could not trace these islands by any accounts or maps in my possession, I named one Chatham Isle, and the other Hood's Island, after the Lords Chatham and Hood... The Redondo is an high barren rock, about a quarter of a mile in circumference, and is visible as far as eight or nine leagues, has soundings round it at the distance of a quarter of a mile thirty fatham. Here our boats caught rock-cod in great abundance. I frequently observed the whales leave these islands and go to the Westward and in a few days, return with augmented numbers. I have also seen the whales coming, as it were, from the main, and passing along from the dawn of day to night in one extended line, as if they were in haste to reach the Galipagoes. It is very much to be regretted that these isles have to this period been so little known but only to the Spaniards... On reaching the South point of

James' Isle, I got sight of three other isles which I had not seen before, nor can I trace them in the Buccaneers' accounts, no more than the isle which we saw to Westward, when at anchor in Stephen's Bay, Chatham Isle. These three isles now seen I named them after the admirals Barrington, Duncan, and Jarvis. The two Northernmost, which are nearest to James' Isle, are the highest, and presented the most agreeable appearance, being covered with trees. The Southernmost, which I named Barrington Isle, is the largest and was the greatest distance from me. It is of a moderate height, and rises in hummocks; the South end is low, running on a parallel with the water's edge. We did not land on either of them. In this expedition we saw great numbers of penguins, and three or four hundred seals. There were also small birds, with a red breast, such as I have seen at the New Hebrides; and others resembling the Java sparrow, in shape and size, but of a black plumage; the male was the darkest, and had a very delightful note. At every place where we landed on the Western side, we might have walked for miles, through long grass and beneath groves of trees. It only wanted a stream to compose a very charming landscape. This isle appears to have been a favourite resort of the Buccaneers, as we not only found seats, which had been made by them of earth and stone, but a considerable number of broken jars scattered about, and some entirely whole, in which the Peruvian wine and liquors of that country are preserved. We also found some old daggers, nails and other implements. This place is, in every respect, calculated for refreshment or relief for crews after a long and tedious voyage, as it abounds with wood, and good anchorage, for any number of ships, and sheltered from all winds by Albemarle Isle.

Colnett named, or renamed, some of the islands, and produced a more modern map than that of Ambrose Cowley (and a better one than Alonso Torres was making at much the same time). Encouraged by the painstaking work of Colnett and his crew, whaling ships soon started to arrive in the Galapagos in greater numbers. They often used the sheltered anchorage at Tagus Cove on Albemarle Island, or a bay on the north side of Charles' Island which the buccaneers and Patrick Watkins had used in their time. The main attraction of this spot was an institution which Colnett seems to have introduced – a primitive post box made of a barrel fixed to a stump. Whaling voyages in those days might well last as long as five years, during which time the captain and crew would be out of touch with the owners and their families. Ships which had just rounded the Horn would leave mail in the box at 'Post Office Bay' to be picked up by other homeward-bound vessels. (This unofficial but practical postal service is still in use today.)

What brought more and more whalers to the South Pacific was, of course, the whales, and what brought the whales was the Humboldt current. Alexander von Humboldt discovered and charted its course in the first years of the nineteenth century, but even before this time seamen knew that a great current swept up the coast from the Antarctic and turned west towards the Galapagos on reaching the latitude of the equator. The cold water was rich enough in plankton to support the huge numbers of whales that Colnett noted, and it brought them with the current towards the Galapagos.

Another factor that brought the whalers and other ships to the islands so regularly was the certainty of a lavish supply of tortoise meat. Fresh meat was practically unknown on very long voyages. In the days before refrigeration, a seaman's normal diet consisted of salt pork in brine, and biscuits which were often rotten with weevils. The giant tortoises not only provided large amounts of meat, but were also easy to catch and could be kept alive for long periods, sometimes a year or more, in the ships' holds without food or water. Almost all who knew the taste of tortoise meat regarded it as a real treat at least in comparison with salt pork. According to one ship's captain of the time, 'The whaling masters seldom care for turtle . . . and generally supply themselves with five hundred or six hundred (tortoises) at a time ... they weigh from one hundred and fifty to three hundred pounds and upwards, that is those they consider fit for their purpose, otherwise they are to be had from half an ounce in weight to six hundred pounds.'

Although a single cargo of six hundred tortoises would not have made any real impact on the huge population, a very much greater number of ships now started frequenting the islands and using the tortoises as a regular source of food. Early visitors had commented that the density of tortoises and iguanas was such that a man had difficulty in avoiding stepping on them but this situation changed tragically. It has been demonstrated from the log books of the American whalers, which formed the largest part of the total whaling fleets, that there were at least seven hundred American whaling ships operating in the Pacific in the years 1811 to 1844. In addition there were the lesser, but still very substantial, number of British and other European whalers, plus the sealers and other vessels which were also using the Galapagos for their supply of meat during this period. The USS *Potomac* recorded that in 1834 no less than thity-one whalers called at Charles' Island alone, which might well have meant that fifteen thousand or more tortoises were taken from that one island. The predictable and terrible result was reported in 1846 by the naturalist on board the British ship, HMS *Herald*. Not a single tortoise was left on Charles' Island. It appears that the tortoise also became extinct at about the same time on Jervis and Barrington Islands. Each of the islands, as we now know, had had a unique subspecies of tortoise. Three of these races were now utterly obliterated.

The whaling industry had much in common with the modern oil industry besides its objectives. The profits of whaling in the nineteenth century were almost as great as those of the Middle Eastern sheikdoms or the Texan oil families of the twentieth century. In both cases the costs of getting these profits were heavy in human suffering, injury and death. Before even starting their hunting in the Pacific, the European and New England whaling ships had to sail round Cape Horn, a dangerous undertaking for any vessel. Having found the whale herd, the crews then had to approach and harpoon their prey from small boats and, once caught, to secure the carcasses and get them on board in conditions which might be hazardous in the extreme. The men who were willing to take ship in the whalers were naturally tough, wild and ungovernable, and the captains who had to lead such crews were inevitably ruthless. Their aim was to kill as many whales as possible with the greatest possible speed, and they were certainly not to be diverted by thoughts about the survival of the species they hunted.

At this time, of course, ecology and ecological balance were ideas unknown to the Western world, and the need for conservation would not have occurred even to civilised and educated people, let alone to the tough and greedy men who made their livings, or their fortunes, from whaling. It was fully accepted then that the natural creation had been put into the world to serve man's purposes and needs. So the whale, like all the rest of created life, could be hunted for its bone, blubber and oil, with a pure Christian conscience. If it had been suggested that the result of indiscriminate exploitation of the sea would be the decimation of its inhabitants, even honest and enlightened men would have replied that this must then be in accord with divine purpose. So the Yankee whalers from New Bedford and Nantucket, and the British and others from still further away, slaughtered the whales with no misgivings and took the precious products home with them for the benefit of their fellow citizens and the shareholders. It is said that the whaling ports of New England in their heyday had the highest per capita wealth of any towns in the world, rivalling San Francisco during the gold rush or Manaus at the height of the Brazilian rubber boom.

Herman Melville, who sailed for years in New England ships, knew the whaling industry as no other writer has done. He described it, or a dramatic version of it, in *Moby Dick*, but passed his own verdict by jumping ship in the Marquesas and living for months among the cannibals there in preference to the hellish life among the whalers. He knew, too, where the proceeds of whaling finally came to rest:

Nowhere in all America will you find more patrician-like houses; park and gardens more opulent than in New Bedford. Whence came they? Go and gaze upon the iron emblematic harpoons round yonder lofty mansions and your question will be answered. All these brave houses and flowery gardens came from the Atlantic, Pacific and Indian Oceans. One and all, they were harpooned and dragged up hither from the bottom of the sea.

The huge but unthinking scale of the whaling holocaust soon brought the industry to an end. Even if we excuse the whalers some of the blame which would be directed now at men who indiscriminately kill off whole species of living creatures, they cannot be exonerated from charges of stupidity. By decimating the spermaceti whale stocks, the Pacific whalers destroyed their own living, just as their contemporaries, the buffalo hunters of North America, were doing. By the end of the American Civil War, the whalers had stopped using the Galapagos.

This, quite coincidentally, reprieved the giant tortoises, which must have been in danger of total extinction by the middle of the nineteenth century. Dr Townsend of the New York Aquarium estimated in 1925 that in one period of thirty years, the whalers took over two hundred thousand. Once the whaling industry switched its attention to the Antarctic the tortoises, on islands where they had survived, were left in peace. Their numbers could then increase again, and the tortoises re-established themselves on seven of the islands. However, all too soon they were threatened from two new directions: introduced animal species, such as rats, dogs, cats, goats, pigs, cattle and donkeys; and another breed of men who were ready to collect these rare animals in large numbers, in the name of science.

Although it is unclear exactly how and when the foreign plants and animals arrived in the islands, there is no doubt of the terrible scale of damage they have done. The nineteenth century saw the indigenous populations of the Galapagos in general retreat in the face of pressure from foreign ones. This problem, and the measures which are at last being taken to halt the process, will be discussed in more detail in Chapter 16.

The attitude of nineteenth-century man to the natural creation in the Galapagos is summed up in a story of the Californian gold rush of the 1850s. The San Francisco newspapers of that time reported the arrival of several ships with cargos of giant tortoises from the Galapagos, to be sold for food to the exploding population of California. For example, in 1855 it is recorded that the schooner *Tarlton* arrived with a cargo of five hundred and eighty tortoises. Ship owners found it profitable to send their vessels south to Peru for supplies of potatoes and onions, and some decided to try to establish a taste for tortoise meat among their customers as well. This trade continued as late as 1902 on a smaller scale. In much the same period scientific expeditions were taking tortoises and specimens of all the other species from the Galapagos, sometimes in almost as great numbers, for the museums and even the private collections of the United States and Europe.

The thoughtless and ruthless approach which seems to have been universally accepted at that time may shock many people today. However, only the educated and relatively wealthy classes in the developed countries can afford these finer feelings even now. The record of supposedly civilised countries in refusing to limit whale catches in the 1980s is shameful proof that greed and short-sighted self-interest are still rampant.

8

The USS Essex

IN 1812 ENGLAND FACED a Europe united against her under Napoleon. From the Balkans to the Arctic and the Atlantic all the major European states except Russia acknowledged Napoleon's suzerainty. The only minor exceptions were Sicily, Sardinia and Sweden, which were passive, and Portugal and part of Spain where the future Duke of Wellington led the only remaining military resistance to Bonaparte. Taking a leaf from the book of the rebellious Irish settlers, the American administration led by President Madison saw an opportunity to profit from England's difficulty. The United States had long objected to the Royal Navy's high-handed practice of impressing sailors from American and other neutral ships, and imposing blockades to prevent trade with Continental ports. Madison decided to seize this moment to strike back against America's former rulers behind the popular rallying cry of 'free trade and sailors' rights'.

The last time England had faced a united Europe and a hostile America (in 1783), she had been forced to accept a peace treaty which freed the United States and set new limits to British power. It was natural for the United States to wish to see Britain humbled again, and to see the British monarchy, which they considered an intolerable tyranny, 'liberalised' by revolutionary France. Fortunately for Madison and his country, they were never obliged to experience the worse tyranny which Bonaparte would have imposed if he had succeeded in defeating the one remaining obstacle to his ambition, England's military and naval power.

The greatest part of that military strength was now engaged in the west of the Spanish peninsula, where Wellington was locked in a life-and-death struggle with the French Imperial Armies. The Royal Navy was deployed on blockade all round the coasts of Western Europe, and, above all, it had to secure the lines of communication and supply through Lisbon of the British, Spanish and Portuguese forces in the Peninsula. However, it could not afford to neglect the vital and vulnerable trade routes to the Caribbean, India, China, the Philippines and Australia, or even the British whaling fleet in the Pacific. Almost all of these maritime targets were now liable to attack, at least in theory, by the small but efficient United States Navy. The sea war was, in fact, mainly fought in the Western Atlantic, where the largest concentrations of British merchantmen sailing to and from the Caribbean were at their most vulnerable, and the United States ships had the greatest relative advantage. It was a war which is remembered chiefly for the burning of Washington by a British force, and for a series of single-ship actions between the two navies: the *Constitution* and the *Java*, the *United States* and the *Macedonian* and, the most famous, the *Chesapeake* and the *Shannon*. At the same time there was a little known campaign on the other side of the continent in which the USS *Essex* under Captain David Porter, based on the Galapagos Islands, captured more than half of the entire British whaling fleet in the Pacific.

Before the outbreak of the war, Captain Porter of the *Essex* was the best known to the English public of all American naval officers, due to various bloodless but vigorous clashes with the Royal Navy. As a youth Porter had been seized by a British press gang in the West Indies and he never forgave this insult. From his grandfather and father he inherited both a nautical tradition and an intense patriotism. His father had fought and been taken prisoner in the

War of American Independence, and he himself had joined the US Navy as a midshipman in 1798. By 1812 he had already seen action in the Caribbean against French and Spanish forces and pirates, as well as a great deal of fighting in the Mediterranean, where he had been captured and held prisoner in Tripoli for some months. Porter hated both his own and his country's enemies, but most of all he hated the British. He was given command of the USS *Essex*, a frigate of 860 tons and forty-four guns, in 1811. The lack of a declaration of war had never prevented him clashing with the British unofficially before, and now he had the benefit of legitimate hostilities as justification for his bellicose spirit.

In October 1812 Porter sailed from the Delaware with orders to join the American Commodore Bainbridge in action against British shipping in the South Atlantic. The arrangements for concentrating the American force there failed, and Porter finally deduced – after posing more than once as a British captain and picking up crucial information in Brazil from the Portuguese authorities – that Bainbridge might never reach their last rendezvous off the Brazilian coast. In his own account of his adventures, David Porter blandly says that at this point 'it became absolutely necessary to depart from the letter of my instructions; I, therefore, determined to pursue that course which seemed to be best calculated to injure the enemy, and would enable me to prolong my cruise.' This meant sailing round Cape Horn into the Pacific on the improbable grounds that the nearest friendly port where fresh supplies could be obtained was Concepción in Chile. In fact Porter had been contemplating this plan of campaign for years and he simply took the first possible opportunity to put it into practice. He rounded the Horn and reached Chile in February 1813. After resting his crew, resupplying and gathering intelligence at Valparaiso, Porter left quickly and sailed northward in the track of the whalers. He reached the Galapagos on April 17th in company with an American whaler, the *Barclay*, whose captain had given Porter more information about both US and British whaling ships in the area. There were no Royal

Navy vessels at all in the Eastern Pacific and thus the *Essex* had a perfect opportunity for offensive action.

His first step was to make for Post Office Bay at Charles' Island, for he knew about the whalers' postal system. He despatched First Lieutenant John Downes, 'to ascertain if any vessels had been lately there, and to bring off such letters as might be of use to us, if he should find any'. He returned in about three hours with several papers, taken from a box which he found nailed to a post, over which was a black sign, on which was a painted 'Hathaway's Post Office'. From this information, Porter was able to deduce a good deal more about the identity and whereabouts of British whalers and to lay his plans for the future. Despite this, there were still two anxious weeks of cruising in and around the islands to be endured. Several times the lookouts shouted 'Sail ho!' only to find that they had been deceived by a rock or an island which looked like a sail.

> There were few on board the ship who did not now despair of making any captures in the Gallipagos Islands; and I believe that many began to think that the information that we had received respecting the practice of British vessels frequenting those islands, as well as the flattering expectations which this information had given rise to, had been altogether deception. But I could not so lightly lay down the opinions, which had caused me to visit those islands, and had been formed on information that could not be doubted. I determined not to leave the Gallipagos so long as there remained a hope of finding a British vessel among them...

Finally on April 29th a genuine sail was sighted and, after a chase, the *Essex* came up with three large British whalers. The first proved to be the *Montezuma* under Captain Baxter, and Porter quickly captured her without a fight by hoisting British colours, a common practice in naval warfare at this time. It would hardly have been possible for any whaling ship to put up a fight against a fully-armed frigate, but any vessel could be taken more expeditiously if caught by surprise, and this was Porter's usual tactic. The *Essex* then resumed the chase for the other two whalers and captured the *Georgiana* (280 tons) and the *Policy* (275 tons), both without bloodshed. Captain Porter's scheme had finally borne fruit:

> The possession of these vessels, besides the great satisfaction it produces, was attended by another advantage of no less importance, as it relieved all our wants except one, to wit, the want of water. From them we obtained an abundant supply of cordage, canvas, paints, tar, and every other article necessary for the ship, of all of which she stood in great need, as our slender stock brought from America had now become worn out and useless. Besides the articles necessary for the ship, we became supplied with a stock of provisions, of a quality and quantity that removed all apprehensions of our suffering for the want of them for many months, as those vessels, when they sailed from England were provided with provisions and stores for upwards of three years, and had not yet consumed half their stock. All were of the best quality; and were it only for the supplying our immediate wants, the prizes were of the greatest importance to us. We found on board of them also wherewith to furnish our crew with several delicious meals. They had been in at James' Island, and had supplied themselves abundantly with those extraordinary animals, tortoises of the Gallipagos, which properly deserve the name of elephant tortoise. Many of them were of a size to weigh upwards of three hundred weight; and nothing, perhaps, can be more disagreeable or clumsy than they are in their external appearance.

Porter put small prize crews under two of his midshipmen into the *Montezuma* and the *Policy*, but he contrived to convert the *Georgiana* into a man-of-war by concentrating all the captured armaments on her and giving her a crew of forty-one under

Lieutenant Downes. He now had two men-of-war under his command and had persuaded some of the crews of the whalers, which contained American as well as British members, that volunteering their services to work their ships was preferable to being kept prisoners.

From that time David Porter's fleet steadily increased. Some of his prizes were sent to the mainland to be sold or to await his arrival in safety; others were armed as auxiliaries. The greatest problem was to find sufficient crews for all the prizes. Before the cruise was ended, the only men above the rank of seaman left on the *Essex* were Porter himself and the surgeon's mate. All the other officers, including the doctor and the chaplain, were detached in command of prize vessels. As a final expediency, Porter appointed a twelve-year-old midshipman called David Farragut to command one of the prizes. This boy, whom Porter had adopted three years previously, was eventually to rise to be the first full admiral of the United States Navy. The midshipman and the youngest officers given these commands were backed up by experienced mates, but it was as well for the security of prizes that the total number taken was not even greater.

In five months of cruising near the Galapagos, Porter captured twelve British whalers, and made the *Essex* the mistress of the Eastern Pacific so conclusively that other vessels made for home prematurely rather than risk the same fate. In most cases, the whalers had sailed straight into Porter's hands as they returned to the Galapagos for fresh provisions, but these apparently easy successes were made possible only by the careful preparation, leadership and organisation which Porter demonstrated throughout his cruise. His losses were remarkably small and, by recruiting from his prizes and American whalers, he actually had more men under his command at the end of the voyage than at the beginning. In his journal, Porter states that by her captures the *Essex*

had completely broken up that important branch of British

navigation, the whale-fishery of the coast of Chili and Peru . . . had deprived the enemy of property to the amount of two and a half millions of dollars and of the services of three hundred and sixty seamen . . . had effectually prevented them from doing any injury to our own whaleships.

It has been argued against him that United States frigates in the Atlantic captured even more prizes in less time. The *Argus*, for example, captured nineteen prizes in thirty-one days while the *Essex* was in the Galapagos. Moreover, the *Essex* now needed refitting and Porter decided to take her to the Marquesas Islands. This visit was a romantic episode involving exotic feasts under coconut palms, Polynesian beauties and even minor wars with the natives, but it made no contribution to the war with Britain. Nevertheless the *Essex*, refitted, careened and resupplied, was ready for further action when she returned to the South American coast at the beginning of 1814. Porter had maintained his ship at sea for nearly eighteen months, his crew was in good health and of high morale, and he had done this without once calling at a home port, a feat of which Drake or Anson would have been proud.

In addition to his exceptional ability as a naval officer, David Porter had the lively mind and the keen eye needed to write an absorbing account of the Galapagos environment and the incidents in which he and his crew were involved there. He described at great length the perpetual struggles he had to find enough water, and how he investigated many novel remedies for scurvy and other diseases:

We were enabled to procure here, also, in large quantities, an herb much resembling spinach, and so called by our people; likewise various other pot-herbs, and prickly pears in great abundance, which were not only of an excellent flavour, but a sovereign anti-scorbutic (cure for scurvy). It afforded me great pleasure to observe that they were so much relished by our people. The cotton plant was found growing spontaneously, and a tree of a very aromatic flavour and taste, which was no other than the one . . . found on the island of Albemarle, and producing in large quantities a resinous substance. This, Mr Adams declared, was the alcornoque, so famous for the cure of consumptions.

He notes that the juice of the prickly pear fruit 'when stewed with sugar made a delicious syrup, while their skins afforded a most excellent preserve, with which we made pies, tarts, etc.' and which helped to keep the men healthy.

He had plenty to say also about the fauna:

The only quadrupeds found on the island were tortoises, lizards, and a few guanas; the land guana was not to be found. Doves peculiar to these islands, of a small size and beautiful plumage, were very numerous and afforded great amusement to the younger part of the crew in killing them with sticks and stones, which was nowise difficulty, as they were very tame. The English mockingbird was also found in great numbers, and a small black bird with a remarkably short and strong bill and a shrill note. These were the only birds except aquatic found here; the latter were not numerous, and consisted of teal, which frequented a lagoon on the east part of the bay, pelicans, boobies, and other birds common to all the islands of these seas. Sea turtles and seals were scarce and shy.

After several weeks in the Galapagos, Porter summed up the water problem:

I have no doubt but the spring formerly mentioned at Charles' Island is a never-failing one, where water may at all times be had; this distance from the sea, to be sure, is great, and but few would attempt to water a ship of war from it; it may, however, be of use to those who are really suffering for water. Colnet and others mention streams of water at James' and Chatham Islands, but I am induced to believe, from what I have learnt from my prisoners, that they owe their existence to temporary rains, and are similar to the place I visited near the basin in Albemarle, where it is said water has been obtained formerly. Supplies from them however, are too precarious to place any dependence on, and it is advisable for every vessel visiting the Gallipagos to lay in good stock of that necessary article, as they may not be so fortunate as myself in capturing vessels with a large quantity on board, which, although contained in the oily casks of a whale-ship, and from them, as may be supposed, derived no very agreeable taste or smell, but on the contrary, produced nausea when drank; yet we considered it the most valuable part of our prize.

He decided to return to the mainland in June, where, after taking three more prizes, he sent Downes south, to Valparaiso, Chile, with four British ships to sell and instructions to rendezvous in the Galapagos thereafter. Porter himself returned there in the *Essex* because of news that three armed British ships had gone there recently to fish. He took them all in a few hours, but even in the excitement of the action he took note of geological happenings:

Notwithstanding the great interest I felt for the critical situation of my prizes, as well as that which every officer must feel when in pursuit of an enemy, I could not help remarking the operations of Nature on the south side of Narborough and on the southern part of Albemarle. Narborough appeared to have undergone great changes since our last visit, by the violent irruptions of its volcanoes; and at this time there were no less than four craters smoking on that island, and one on the south part of Albemarle. I should have before mentioned, that a few hours after leaving Charles' Island, a volcano burst out with great fury from its centre, which would naturally lead to the belief of a submarine communication between them.

One of the British armed whalers, the *Sir Andrew Hammond*, succeeded in getting away from the *Essex* after each captain had confused the other by flying his opponent's colours and the British had outrowed the Americans in a contest lasting many hours. Six weeks later the *Essex* managed to capture the same whaler, also commanded, as it proved, by a Captain Porter. Neither captain recognised his opponent until they had closed because both ships had so altered their appearances in the meanwhile in the hope of deceiving the other. From this prize, too, David Porter got an unexpected bonus:

> What was more acceptable to our men than all the rest, I took from her two puncheons of choice Jamaica spirits which was greatly relished... Whether it was the great strength of the rum, or the length of time they had been without I cannot say: but our seamen were so affected by the first allowance served out to them that many were taken to their hammocks perfectly drunk. Considering . . . the great propensity of seamen for spirituous liquors, and as no evil was likely to result from a little inebrity... I felt disposed to give them a little latitude, which in no instance was productive of unpleasant consequences.

In more modern times the American navy would have had nothing to do with 'spirituous liquors' on its ships, but in Porter's day it still followed the bad old ways of its English progenitor. Another practice which is inconceivable nowadays in either navy but was still current then was the duel. Porter records 'with the utmost pain' the death of a promising young lieutenant shot at the third fire as a result of 'a practice which disgraces human nature'. He was buried on the shore of James' Island where he had died, and the following was erected over the grave: 'Sacred to the memory of Lieut. John S. Cowan of the US Frigate *Essex* who died here anno 1813, Aged 21 years.' The officer who duelled with and shot Cowan was Lieutenant Gamble of the Marines, who was to distinguish himself much more admirably by successfully navigating a prize vessel from the Marquesas on an epic voyage of thousands of kilometres to the Sandwich Islands (now called Hawaii) with a crew of only two able-bodied men.

When Captain Porter left the Marquesas he returned to Valparaiso with the *Essex* and one armed prize, *Essex Junior*, where he knew he would find the British frigate HMS *Phoebe* under Captain Hillyar, and the sloop HMS *Cherub*. After some discussion ashore between Porter and Hillyar, they agreed to avoid any action or gunfire in Valparaiso harbour because it might easily have harmed innocent civilians or their property.

Hillyar put to sea and for a month covered the harbour with his two ships, hoping that Porter would emerge to fight. Having slightly the inferior force, Porter now tried to find some means of evening the odds but failed. Eventually, he was obliged by a sudden storm to leave the safety of the roadstead, the engagement took place and the *Essex*, after taking appalling losses, was forced to surrender. Hillyar and Porter subsequently agreed to neutralize the *Essex Junior*, and the American prisoners on parole, including Porter and David Farragut, were returned to the United States in her.

David Porter's later career was as colourful as the cruise of the *Essex* had been. He was continually at odds with his superiors, even with Congress, and eventually resigned in order to become commander-in-chief of the Mexican Navy in the war of liberation with Spain. However, he found it even harder to serve a foreign government. Finally, he was appointed United States Minister at Constantinople, where he died. Diplomacy may seem a strange occupation for so fierce an individualist, but in the days before telegraph or wireless communication a diplomat posted thousands of kilometres away from his government could enjoy almost as much independence as a naval captain commanding a ship such as the *Essex*.

Captain Porter's exploits in the *Essex* may seem irrelevant in the context of the great battles sweeping to a climax in the Iberian peninsula and on the plains of Russia. Napoleon and his armies were being faced and beaten for the first time in two decades, and the campaigns were to change the balance of power in Europe for half a century. However, Porter's solitary cruise was a classic demonstration of the use of sea power. Even when the power is slight, mobility and its dividend of surprise give that power a disproportionate impact. To counter the *Essex*'s presence in the Pacific Britain had to divert two ships, *Phoebe* and *Cherub*, from vital tasks, and while the fate of an Empire hung in the balance in Europe, send them to another ocean on a mission which took half a year to complete. This lesson was never forgotten by the United States Navy. The fact that Porter eventually lost his ship and returned home as a prisoner on parole subtracts nothing from the reputation he earned in the Galapagos.

9

Visitors and Settlers

THE REPORTS PUBLISHED by Captains Colnett and Porter proved to the world at large that, apart from its reptiles, no great natural resources were to be found in the Galapagos. After the liberation of the South American continent from Spanish rule in the 1820s, the islands had fewer strategic attractions. Traders could use the mainland ports quite freely, and any ship with legitimate business could resupply more conveniently, if more expensively, in those ports. Nevertheless visitors continued to arrive for various purposes, some of which were as strange as the islands themselves.

Once the Napoleonic wars were over the Royal Navy resumed the eighteenth-century practice of detaching its ships from time to time on lengthy cruises in remote parts of the world. From 1820 to 1822, Captain Basil Hall sailed up and down the coasts of Chile, Peru and Mexico in HMS *Conway*, engaged in a variety of political, geographical and scientific tasks. At the end of 1821, after spending a convivial Christmas in Guayaquil, he sailed to Abingdon Island, where he spent two weeks, suffering as usual from water shortages. The purpose of his visit was to conduct experiments as near as possible to the equatorial line 'with an invariable pendulum of Captain Kater's construction'. One might think that these experiments could have been carried out as well or better on the mainland, but doubtless Basil Hall was making the best of his opportunities to travel.

Another Royal Navy officer arrived in the archipelago soon after on an even more peculiar mission. In 1824 King Tamehamelia II, of the Sandwich Islands, and his Queen, fascinated by the stories they had heard from English visitors to their islands about the wonders of their kingdom, accepted an invitation to pay a visit to the British Isles. Unhappily, the visitors had no resistance to English germs, and both caught measles and died within a week of each other. The British Government had promised its protection to the Sandwich Islands, and hoping to salvage something from the wreck of this state visit, determined to send the royal remains to their own home to rest. The task was given to Captain The Right Honourable Lord Byron, and he decided, partly for the usual practical reasons and no doubt partly from a proper curiosity, to put in at the Galapagos on the long haul from Cape Horn to the Sandwich Islands. The two teak coffins which HMS *Blonde* was carrying were no longer a pleasant cargo, but a few more days could make no difference. On March 25th, 1825 she anchored at Tagus, or Banks' Cove on Albemarle Island. As befitted the son of a poet, Lord Byron recorded his impressions in vivid language:

The place is like a new creation; the birds and beasts do not get out of our way; the pelicans and sea-lions look in our faces as if we had no right to intrude on their solitude; the small birds are so tame that they hop upon our feet; and all this amidst volcanoes which are burning round us on either hand. Altogether it is as wild and desolate a scene as imagination can picture.

Our party to Narborough Island landed among an innumerable host of sea-guanas, the ugliest living creatures we ever beheld. They are like the alligator but with a more hideous head and of a dirty sooty black colour, and sat on the black lava rocks like so many imps of darkness. As far as the eye could reach we saw nothing but rough fields of lava, that seemed to have hardened while the force of the wind had been rippling its liquid surface. About halfway down the steep southeast side of the Island, a volcano burns day and night; and near the beach a crater was pouring forth streams of lava, which on reaching the sea caused it to bubble in an extraordinary manner.

These eruptions on Narborough Island had by good chance been witnessed at their peak and described in graphic detail by yet another visitor only a month before. This was Benjamin Morrell, the captain of the New York-based schooner *Tartar*, who made many memorable voyages and wrote about them in the full-blown prose of his time.

14 February. On Monday the fourteenth, at two o'clock a.m. while the sable mantle of night was yet spread over the mighty Pacific, shrouding the neighbouring islands from our view, and while the stillness of death reigned everywhere about us, our ears were suddenly assailed by a sound that could only be equalled by ten thousand thunders bursting upon the air at once; while, at the same instant, the whole hemisphere was lighted up with a horrid glare that might have appalled the stoutest heart! I soon ascertained that one of the volcanoes of Narborough Island, which had quietly slept for the last ten years, had suddenly broke forth with accumulated vengeance...

The sublimity, the majesty, the terrific grandeur of this scene baffle description and set the powers of language at defiance. Had the first of Milton's hell burst its vault of adamant, and threatened the heavens with conflagration, his description of the incident would have been appropriate to the present subject. No words that I can command will give the reader even a faint idea of the awful splendour of the great reality.

Had it been the 'crack of doom' that aroused them, my men could not have been sooner on deck, where they stood gazing like 'sheeted spectres', speechless and bewildered with astonishment and dismay. The heavens appeared to be one blaze of fire, intermingled with millions of falling stars and meteors; while the flames shot upward from the peak of Narborough to the height of at least two thousand feet in air. All hands soon became sensible of the cause of the startling phenomenon, and on recovering from their first panic could contemplate its progress with some degree of composure.

But the most splendid and interesting scene of this spectacle was yet to be exhibited. At about half-past four o'clock a.m. the boiling contents of the tremendous caldron had swollen to the brim, and poured over the edge of the crater in a cataract of liquid fire. A river of melted lava was now seen rushing down the side of the mountain, pursuing a serpentine course to the sea, a distance of about three miles from the blazing orifice of the volcano. This dazzling stream descended in a gully, one-fourth of a mile in width, presenting the appearance of a tremendous torrent of melted iron running from the furnace. The demon of fire seemed rushing to the embraces of Neptune; and dreadful indeed was the uproar occasioned by their meeting. The ocean boiled and roared and bellowed, as if a civil war had broken out in the Tartarean gulf.

At three a.m. I ascertained the temperature of the water, by Fahrenheit's thermometer, to be 61°, while that of the air was 71°. At eleven a.m., the air was 113° and the water 100°, the eruption still continuing with unabated fury. The *Tartar*'s anchorage was about ten miles to the northward of the mountain, and the heat was so great that the melted pitch was running from the vessel's seams, and the tar dropping from the rigging...

In order to give the reader a correct idea of our situation, it will be necessary to remind him of the relative position of these two islands. Albemarle Island is the most extensive of the whole Galapagos group, being about ninety miles in length from north to south, narrow and nearly straight on its eastern shore; but on the western side it hollows in from Christopher's point on the south, to Cape Berkley on the north; and within this space lies the island of Narborough, its eastern point approaching nearest to Albemarle. The *Tartar* lay in a cove of Banks' Bay, on the western shore of Albemarle, directly opposite the northeast point of Narborough; and this cove could be approached from the northwest through Banks' Bay, or from the southwest through Elizabeth Bay.

Our situation was every hour becoming more critical and alarming. Not a breath of air was stirring to fill a sail, had we attempted to escape; so that we were compelled to remain idle and unwilling spectators of a pyrotechnic exhibition which evinced no indications of even a temporary suspension. All that day the fires continued to rage with unabating activity, while the mountain still continued to belch forth its melted entrails in an unceasing cataract. The mercury continued to rise till four p.m., when the temperature of the air had increased to 123°, and that of the water to 105°. Our respiration now became difficult, and several of the crew complained of extreme faintness.

It was evident that something must be done and that promptly. 'O for a cap-full of wind!' was the prayer of each. The breath of a light zephyr from the continent, scarcely perceptible to the cheek, was at length announced as the welcome signal for the words, 'All hands, unmoor!' This was a little before eight p.m. The anchor was soon apeak, and every inch of canvas extended along the spars, where it hung in useless drapes.

All was again suspense and anxious expectation. Again the zephyr breathed and hope revived. At length it was announced from aloft that the lighter canvas began to feel the air; and in a few minutes more top-sails began gradually to fill, when the anchor was brought to the bow, and the *Tartar* began to move. At eight o'clock we were wafted by a fine little easterly breeze, for which we felt grateful to Heaven.

Our course lay southward, though the little strait or sound that separated the burning mountain from Albemarle Island; my object being to get to windward of Narborough as soon as possible. It is true that the northwest passage from Banks' Bay, by Cape Berkley, would have been a shorter route to the main ocean; but not the safest, under existing circumstances. I therefore chose to run south, to Elizabeth Bay, though in doing so we had to pass within about four miles of those rivers of flaming lava, which were pouring into the waters of the bay. Had I adopted the other course, and passed to the leeward of Narborough, we might have got clear of the island, but it would have been impossible to prevent the sails and rigging taking fire; as the whole atmosphere on the lee side of the bay appeared to be one mass of flame. The deafening sounds accompanying the eruption still continued; indeed the terrific grandeur of the scene would have been incomplete without it.

Heaven continued to favour us with a fine breeze, and the *Tartar* slid along through the almost boiling ocean at the rate of about seven miles an hour. On passing the currents of melted lava, I became apprehensive that I should lose some of my men, as the influence of the heat was so great that several of them were incapable of standing. At that time the mercury in the thermometer was at 147° but on immersing it in water, it instantly rose to 150°. Had the wind deserted us here, the consequences must have been horrible. But the mercy of Providence was still extended toward us, the refreshing breeze still urged us forward towards a more temperate atmosphere; so that at eleven p.m. we were safely anchored at the south extremity of the bay, while the flaming Narborough lay fifteen miles to the leeward.

With foreign visitors bringing back this kind of tale from the islands, it is not surprising that few others wished to go, let alone to settle there. However, the second decade of the century was a time of revolutionary upheaval throughout Latin America and, whatever foreigners thought, the leading spirits of the liberation movement believed that a new era was dawning in which many great developments would prove possible. In 1824 the last source of Spanish power on the continent was overthrown when the Royalist forces in Peru were defeated at the Battle of Ayacucho. The independent republics of Peru and Gran Colombia were established in the same year, and the latter split into Venezuela, Colombia and Ecuador in 1830. With the political map of South America being redrawn in this drastic way, all sorts of new opportunities were emerging for men with the imagination to see them and one of them was bound to conceive the idea of colonising the Galapagos Islands. This scheme was the brainchild of General José Villamil, son of a wealthy family in Louisiana, which was a Spanish colony until 1803. Villamil had achieved some military distinction in the wars of liberation and then established himself in Guayaquil, which was, and remains, the largest city and main port of Ecuador. There he launched his 'Sociedad Colonizadora del Archipiélago de Galapagos' with the authority of the government.

Until then the status of the Galapagos islands had not been a subject which occupied the minds of politicians very often. In theory, the papal bull of 1493 awarded sovereignty over these, as over all Pacific islands, to Spain, but the Spanish authorities in Panama and Lima had never bothered to confirm ownership of these apparently useless and mainly barren islands. Now that there might be some possibility of dispute about them between the new republics of Colombia, Ecuador and Peru, the Ecuadorians, prompted by Villamil, sent a representative party to the islands to proclaim the archipelago part of Ecuador on February 12th, 1832. This ceremony was conducted by Colonel Ignacio Hernández, who had been appointed Justice of the Peace for the new territory, and it was attended by a number of witnesses, including the crews of two American whalers which happened to be at Charles' Island at the time.

Colonel Hernández' first official act was the courteous but possibly confusing gesture of renaming Charles' Island as Floreana, after the first President of the Republic of Ecuador, General Juan José Flores. This name persisted but, perhaps fortunately, Hernandez' attempts to rename more islands after other prominent Ecuadorians failed. The new republic's title to the Galapagos islands was never challenged by the neighbouring states which might have had some claim to them. In 1840 Ecuador signed a treaty with Spain in which the transfer of Sovereignty was recognised by the former colonial power which had held it, if a little absentmindedly, for nearly 350 years.

The formal proclamation of Ecuador's sovereignty over the archipelago mentions the name of Juan Johnson as a witness, and describes him as an old inhabitant of Charles' Island. Presumably he was the only permanent inhabitant, Patrick Watkins having left some twenty years before, but he was now joined by the first colonists brought in by General Villamil. Lacking an adequate number of people of substance, these turned out to be a group of eighty Ecuadorian soldiers, who had been condemned to death for mutiny and reprieved by the General on condition that they were deported to Galapagos to work the lands of his colonising association there. The General himself was appointed Governor General of the territory. When he took up residence he brought with him a number of artisans and farmers, who had better qualifications for pioneering work than the majority of the mutinous soldiers would have had. The number of colonists was also increased after 1833 when the government in Quito started to send out political dissenters banished from the mainland.

Creating a durable settlement populated by mutineers and political exiles would have been problematic enough to sink most projects of this kind, and Villamil's difficulties could not have been alleviated when the islands started to be used also as a penal settlement for ordinary criminals and a dumping ground for prostitutes deported from Guayaquil. For a time, however, the colony seems to have prospered. Its principal settlement was at Charles' Island on productive land with an adequate water supply, about 8 kilometres from the shore and 300 metres above sea level, and this was optimistically christened 'Haven of Peace'. Here corn, potatoes and sugar could be grown and domestic animals raised to supplement the population of wild goats and pigs, which had certainly been established there in David Porter's time and possibly much longer.

The principal purpose of Villamil's enterprise was to try to develop a new natural resource which had been discovered on some of the islands, especially on Charles' Island – orchilla or dyer's moss (*Rocella tinctoria*). Villamil hoped to get a good return by exporting it for the manufacture of dyes, and various efforts were made to develop this trade, but none had more than temporary success. The only steady profit to be made in the Galapagos still seemed to come through supplying fresh fruit, vegetables and other foodstuffs to the whalers, as Patrick Watkins had done in his time. In so far as the permanent Ecuadorian settlers succeeded in making a living at more than subsistence level, it was probably by selling to whalers on the spot rather than by the export of orchilla.

By 1835 the permanent population of the archipelago was probably between two and three hundred. On September 15th of that year the most famous of all visitors to the Galapagos arrived, when HMS *Beagle*, commanded by Captain Robert FitzRoy and with the young Charles Darwin on board as naturalist, anchored at Chatham Island. The governor, disillusioned perhaps by the decline of enthusiasm for his projects, was not in residence and it was his deputy, an Englishman called Lawson, who showed Darwin round the settlement on Charles' Island. A chance remark of Lawson's about tortoises started a new train of thought in Darwin's mind and gave Lawson, of whom we know nothing else, a sort of scientific immortality.

Darwin's curiosity and industry in recording everything of interest compelled him to describe the settlement in his diary:

The houses are scattered over the cultivated ground and form what in Chili would be called a 'Pueblo' (village). Since leaving Brazil we have not seen so Tropical a Landscape, but there is a great deficiency in the absence of the lofty, various and all-beautiful trees of that country... It appears that the people are far from contented, they complain, here as in Chiloé (Southern Chile), of the deficiency of money: I presume there is some more essential want than that of mere currency, namely want of sale of their produce... The inhabitants here lead a sort of Robinson Crusoe life; the houses are very simple, built of poles and thatched with grass. Part of their time is employed in hunting the wild pigs and goats with which the woods abound; from the climate agriculture requires but a small portion. The main article is the Terrapin or Tortoise; such numbers yet remain, that it is calculated two days' hunting will find food for the other five in the week...

Darwin paints a picture of a life which was anything but idyllic, and unlikely to attract or retain voluntary settlers for very long. There was certainly no sign that Villamil's plans for a prosperous orchilla export trade were proving successful. We shall see later what was in store for this first settlement in the archipelago, but Darwin claims attention first.

10

Darwin in the Galapagos

WHEN CHARLES DARWIN arrived in the Galapagos he was twenty-six, having left England as an immature twenty-two-year-old in 1831 – a surprising choice to be invited to join Captain FitzRoy in HMS *Beagle* as supernumerary, unpaid naturalist. His father, Dr Robert Darwin of Shrewsbury, was already greatly disappointed in the young Charles and worried about his future. Exasperated with his son on one occasion he had burst out: 'You care for nothing but shooting, dogs and rat-catching, and you will be a disgrace to yourself and all your family.'

On finishing school Charles had been sent to study medicine at Edinburgh University with the idea of following in his father's footsteps. However, he could not stand the tedium of the Edinburgh academics' medical lectures, and complained bitterly of them in letters home to his sisters: 'Dr Duncan is so very learned that his wisdom has left no room for his sense, he lectures . . . on the Materia Medica, which cannot be translated into any words expressive enough of its stupidity.' Nor could he stomach being present at dissections and surgical operations, which must, indeed, have been excruciating ordeals even for the onlooker, performed as they were without anaesthetic. After two years the worried doctor accepted that medicine would not hold his son, and suggested that he go up to Cambridge instead to read divinity with the idea of his becoming a clergyman.

As an intellectual diet divinity did not stimulate Charles' mind any more than scientific studies. He enjoyed himself, as he always had done at home in Shrewsbury, in all kinds of country pursuits. He loved shooting partridges and tells us in his autobiography that up to at least 1831 'I should have thought myself mad to give up the first days of Partridge shooting (in September) for geology or any other science.' He had always enjoyed collecting insects, flowers and rocks and continued this interest in Cambridge as he scraped unethusiastically through a pass degree in divinity. The life of a country parson might have been pleasant enough to satisfy Charles Darwin, and it is easy to image him settling down, like Gilbert White at Selborne, to a quiet life centred on local and parish matters, allowing him unlimited opportunity for the study of nature in the English countryside of that peaceful age. However, Charles at this time was threatening to turn into a bit of a waster. He had great charm, was loved by his relations and made friends easily, but in the modern idiom, he was not motivated, and despite his great natural advantages, was in danger of drifting into an aimless and unsatisfying life.

Yet, unnoticed by Charles himself or his father, interests and abilities were stirring in him. At Edinburgh he followed the course on geology, despite finding the lectures tiresome. He spent hours in the university museum, becoming a friend of its director, and he was taught to stuff birds and animals by a negro who knew South America. At Cambridge he kept up his interest in geology, and Professor Adam Sedgwick thought enough of him to invite him on a field expedition in Wales. He also became close friends with the Reverend Professor John Henslow, an eminent botanist.

At this time Captain FitzRoy was looking for a naturalist to accompany the survey ship HMS *Beagle* on a hydrographical voyage to South America and back home across the Pacific. The first choice for this position was Professor Henslow, but his wife objected understandably to losing her husband for several years on end – five as it transpired – and Henslow recommended that Darwin should go instead.

Henslow was an established professional scientist at Cambridge, already the centre of most English natural sciences, whereas Darwin was destined for the church but not yet fully qualified for holy orders, let alone for the role of naturalist on this extraordinary voyage. There were many other experienced naturalists with proper qualifications to take advantage of the unusual and splendid opportunity offered by the *Beagle*. The young Darwin did not even have the ambition to become a professional scientist; he thought of his interest in geology, botany and biology purely as hobbies. There must have been a quality in his approach to science which experienced professionals such as Sedgwick and Henslow recognised, for they would not have taken any notice of this untried beginner otherwise. None of the older men who knew Charles Darwin in those early years has left any written testament of what it was about him that caught and held their attention. However, once he set forth in HMS *Beagle*, everyone who knew him (and we who can read the diary and journals that he wrote at the time) quickly appreciated his talents.

Before this could happen there were a number of hurdles to cross. First Dr Darwin had to be convinced that his son would benefit by a protracted trip round the world in pursuit of interests which were merely a hobby. 'Bug hunting' was not a good preparation for the church. The rather formidable doctor was firmly opposed to Henslow's suggestion and Charles actually wrote to Henslow to refuse. However, he was lucky to have an outstandingly far-sighted uncle in Josiah Wedgwood, of the famous Wedgwood Pottery, who immediately realised that this was an opportunity which could be a turning point in a young man's life. He tackled the sceptical father and persuaded him to continue Charles' allowance for the duration of the voyage, which they seem naively to have thought would not be a lengthy one. Young Charles

Darwin's name was, therefore, submitted to Captain FitzRoy as suitable to be the *Beagle*'s naturalist by Professor Henslow, but it was by no means certain that FitzRoy would accept him.

FitzRoy's was a strange and difficult character, in many ways the opposite of Darwin's. He was an aristocrat, a Tory and an authoritarian, while the Darwins were upper-class Whigs or liberals, and mildly intellectual. After his remarkable personal achievement as navigator, seaman and hydrographer, FitzRoy went on to fill a number of naval and civil posts, including a brief and unfortunate spell of two years as Governor of New Zealand, and became a vice-admiral. Later still he found his niche and vocation as the first and pioneering head of the Meteorological Office. While an innovator in technical matters and a man of considerable intellect, he became in later life a rock-hard Christian fundamentalist. There was in him a dichotomy between the outwardly conventional and rigid naval officer, and a restless inner personality which expressed itself in acts of great generosity and human sympathy. FitzRoy also swung between moods of elation and depression, and these became more marked as he got older until in 1865, affected by criticism of his work at the Meteorological Office, he became so deeply depressed that he cut his own throat. However, while the preparations for the *Beagle*'s new voyage were going along in 1831, FitzRoy's only obvious fault was a hot temper.

According to his own account, FitzRoy wanted 'some well-educated and scientific person . . . who would willingly share such accommodations as I had to offer, in order to profit by the opportunity of visiting distant countries yet little known.' He had in mind particularly a 'scientific person' with knowledge of minerology and geology but it seems likely that he was happy to accept the academic qualifications of whoever might be recommended by the dons at Cambridge. As important no doubt for both men was that they should get on well, since they would have to share a tiny cabin for months and years on end. Apparently, FitzRoy was doubtful at first that Darwin would be an agreeable cabin-mate mainly because he disapproved of the shape of his nose and was a firm believer in judging character by physiognomy. Darwin's engaging manners, his enthusiasm and his own immediate respect for FitzRoy quickly overcame the bad impression created by his nose, however, and the two men got on well. Since FitzRoy's temper was uncertain and his depressive tendency emerged at times during the voyage there were naturally moments of stress, but overall their relations prospered and developed into friendship. Indeed, the long discussions which they had in the next five years about the nature of the world and its creation were a vital part of the process of discovery.

It is not always realised that FitzRoy was an active participant in the intellectual treasure hunt on which Darwin embarked. Some authorities (such as de Beer, Mellesh, Moorehead and Chancellor) believed that FitzRoy wanted his geologist to provide the evidence which would substantiate the truth of the Book of Genesis, physical proof of the Flood, or even of the first appearance of created things on Earth. Darwin, clergyman-to-be as well as scientist, was uniquely qualified to do this. However, the evidence of FitzRoy's own writing, *Narrative of the Surveying Voyages of HMS* Adventure *and* Beagle *between 1826 and 1836*, indicates that he had not taken up his extreme fundamentalist, or creationist, view until at least the end of the voyage. In 1831, it may well have been Darwin, with his more recent conventional education, his theological studies and his presumed vocation for the Church, who was more inclined to accept the literal truth of the Book of Genesis. If this is so, it is a strange irony that as Darwin slowly came to envisage a different origin for all natural life, FitzRoy's mind, exposed to all the same evidence and argument, moved ever more decisively in the opposite direction.

Charles Darwin knew as soon as FitzRoy accepted him that he had reached a turning point in life. 'There is indeed a tide in the affairs of men,' he wrote to his sister Susan, 'and I have experienced it.' He saw the years ahead of him, as any young man would, as a chance to see the known world and explore some of its unknown parts, an intensely romantic prospect. He could not then begin to envisage how the experience of the voyage of the *Beagle* would eventually lead him to revolutionise scientific thought with a new theory of the origin of species. However, he was intellectually better prepared than might have been expected. While he had given as little real attention as he could to medicine and theology, he had read widely in the fields which truly interested him, Fleming's *Philosophy of Zoology*, Burchell's *Travels*, Scrope on *Volcanoes* and Caldcleugh's *Travels in South America*, and knew something of the evolutionary thinking of the French scientists Lamarck and Buffon. He also, of course, knew the writings of his own grandfather, Erasmus Darwin, whose visionary ideas about evolution and other novel theories had been described as 'darwinising' by the poet Coleridge. Later in life Charles Darwin said that he had been little, if at all, influenced by the theories of his grandfather or of these other predecessors. He did, however, readily and humbly acknowledge his debt to a contemporary, Charles Lyell, whose newly published work *Principles of Geology* fundamentally changed thinking on that subject. He took the first volume of Lyell's book with him when the *Beagle* sailed, and the second was sent out to him in South America as soon as it came off the press. He also had with him the personal narrative of one of his most distinguished forerunners, Alexander von Humboldt. More importantly Darwin had the priceless benefit of what his uncle Josiah Wedgwood had called 'an enlarged curiosity'. It was this inexorably enquiring spirit and his powers of observation which were the moving forces driving him onward. From Henslow and Sedgwick, Darwin had learned the basis of scientific field work. Now Lyell's example of patient and methodical collection and evaluation of facts as a preliminary to all speculation showed him the right method to use.

HMS *Beagle* made her landfall at Chatham Island on September 15th, 1835. For most of her crew this was just another routine port of call. The Galapagos did not offer the varied attractions and absorbing or beautiful scenery which they had enjoyed over the two years and more they had already spent surveying the shores of South America, nor were they lush, tropical lands like the Society Islands which were to be visited next. These islands had little to recommend them except that they were 'infinitely strange, unlike any other islands in the world'. As the *Beagle* approached Chatham, they saw a shore of hideous black lava that had been twisted and tossed about as though it were a stormy sea petrified at a stroke. 'A shore,' said FitzRoy, 'fit for pandemonium.' When Darwin was finally able to land two days later, it made the same impression on him: 'Nothing could be less inviting than the first appearance. A broken field of black, basaltic lava . . . crossed by great fissures, is everywhere covered by stunted sunburnt brushwood . . . the many craters vividly reminded me of parts of Staffordshire where the great iron foundries are most numerous.' Thoughts of 'dark Satanic mills' suggest that the islands did not appear earthly at all, but more like ante-chambers to hell.

The *Beagle's* anchorage at Chatham Island offered some better cheer for the crew. They found that innumerable tropical fish, sharks and turtles swarmed round the ship, 'popping their heads up in all quarters', and could be caught as fast as lines could be thrown to them. 'This spot,' Darwin noted, 'makes all hands very easy; loud laughter and the heavy flapping of fish are heard on every side.' An American whaler, the *Science*, a magnificent vessel with nine whale boats aboard, shared the same anchorage at St Stephen's Harbour. There were thus some other friendly souls with whom to wonder at the extraordinary natural life to be seen in this infernal landscape. Parties landing to explore the foreshore found the black sand so hot that it burnt their feet even through thick boots. They were enthralled by the sight of giant tortoises 'shuffling and waddling about in the soft clayey soil near a spring'. Some of these were so large that when standing on their four legs they reached the breast of a man. Darwin wrote in his diary:

These islands appear paradise for the whole family of Reptiles… The Tortoise is so abundant that [a] single ship's company have caught 500–800 in a short time. The black lava rocks on the beach are frequented by large (2–3ft) most disgusting, clumsy lizards. They are as black as the porous rocks over which they crawl and seek their prey from the sea. Somebody calls them 'imps of darkness'. They assuredly well become the land they inhabit.

The *Beagle* spent just five weeks in the archipelago, and her itinerary took her to most of the principal islands. Darwin was not able to land on all of them as many days were spent at sea sounding and surveying the coasts, but he went ashore with his servant, Covington, to collect and observe as intensively as he could at every possible opportunity. The islands at which he made fairly protracted visits were Chatham (September 17th–22nd), Charles' (24th–27th September), Albemarle (September29th–October 2nd) and James' (October 8th–17th).

At Charles' Island, the main focus of interest was the settlement which the acting governor, Lawson, took Darwin and his companions to visit. At Albemarle, and even more at Narborough Island, his thoughts and powers of observation were aimed, as they had been primarily throughout the earlier part of the voyage, at determining the geology of what he saw. His diary and journal concentrate on the lava formations and the ever-threatening volcanoes.

However, he spent the most time on James' Island camping on shore for a whole week with the ship's surgeon, Benjamin Bynoe, and three sailors. Here the most striking feature was the fauna and all the creatures they observed were odd in different ways. There were flightless cormorants, and creatures belonging to cold seas, such as penguins and seals, which were living in the tropics for no conceivable reason. The marine 'lizards' proved to be miniature dragons or iguanas, which grew to an average length of 0.9 to 1.2

metres. They even breathed vapour from their nostrils, but it turned out to be brine and not fire. Darwin and Bynoe opened up the stomach of one to discover that they ate seaweed and nothing else.

Darwin saw marine iguanas cruising close to the sea bottom and found that they could stay submerged for a long time; a sailor threw one into the sea with a weight attached to it and found it alive and kicking when he pulled it up more than an hour later. Yet this strange animal seemed to fear the sea; when Darwin threw one out into deep water, it promptly swam back to shore and it did the same each time it was thrown into the sea. Darwin concluded that it instinctively feared attack by sharks or seals in its true element, and sought safety on shore where it usually had no enemies.

The land iguanas were a completely different species, even uglier than their marine cousins. They were more vividly coloured, yellowy orange and brick red in blotches, but looked menacing and had sharp teeth. In those days there were so many land iguanas on James' that Darwin and his party had difficulty finding a space free from burrows on which to pitch their tent. Fortunately, the iguanas never seemed to want to attack men. When Darwin pulled one by its tail out of its burrow, it turned round and eyed him indignantly as if to say 'Why did you pull my tail?' Nevertheless, when thrown a piece of cactus (their staple food) they were quick enough to quarrel over it, tugging it away from each other like dogs worrying a bone.

The other creatures which subsisted on cactus were the giant tortoises. They, too, offered no threat despite their size, nor had they any means of defending themselves except to draw in their heads and sink to the ground. The larger ones were so big and heavy that Darwin and Covington found it impossible to lift them or even to turn them over on to their backs, the accepted way of capturing them. These giants could easily bear a man's weight, and when Darwin mounted on one it did not even seem to notice his presence. He calculated that it would cover something like 360 yards in an hour or three miles in a day.

When Darwin and his companions climbed away from the shore zone towards the higher parts of the island, they discovered the origin of the paths through the underbrush which they had first noticed in Chatham Island. They were made by tortoises plodding uphill to a freshwater spring. The men found that there was a two-way traffic, some tortoises going up to drink while others passed them coming down again. The procession continued endlessly, and might have been going on forever.

As they climbed higher, Darwin found himself in very different terrain. The garua clouds met the land, providing moisture which hardly ever reached the coastal strip only a short distance away. It was the garua – a light drizzle or scotch mist – rather than water from the spring which caused trees to grow tall and covered them with ferns, lichens and mosses. However, it was to the spring that the tortoises headed 'with all deliberate speed' and where, Darwin noted, regardless of spectators or anything else, they plunged their heads into the water swallowing great mouthfuls at the rate of ten in a minute. 'Near the spring,' he wrote, 'it was a curious spectacle to behold many of these huge creatures, one set eagerly travelling onwards with outstretched necks and another set returning, having drunk their fill.' The tortoises seemed to drink and drink insatiably. They might, in fact, have to take in enough to last them for a month or more. On islands where water was available, the tortoises would travel miles for it, and spend hours wallowing in the mud round the springs. But they could survive even on the smaller, waterless islands where they seemed able to satisfy their thirst, as seamen had done when need be, by sucking the moisture from the pads of cactus leaves.

At the time of Darwin's visit the tortoise population of Charles' Island was declining all too fast. Having the best-known water supply, this island was most used by the whalers, and the newly-established Ecuadorian settlement also fed itself to a very large extent on tortoise meat. While camping on James', Darwin and his party lived entirely on tortoise meat, which they found palatable enough when roasted in the shell 'as the Gauchos do' or made into a delicious soup. Certainly they thought this a better diet than iguanas: 'These lizards, when cooked, yield a white meat which is liked by those whose stomachs soar above all prejudices.' Darwin's stomach was obviously not free from prejudice but he remains marvellously objective when he adds: 'Humboldt has remarked that in the inter-tropical America all lizards which inhabit dry regions are esteemed delicacies for the table.'

Passing back from gastronomic to scientific observations, Darwin noticed that the tortoise's bladder served as a reservoir in which to store the water it would need for long periods. He proved this by discovering that the inhabitants, when overcome by thirst in a dry zone or island, would kill a tortoise and drink the water so stored. Darwin tried this himself and found that the fluid was 'quite limpid and with only a slightly bitter taste.' He observed that the tortoises were deaf and could not hear anything approaching them from behind. During the breeding season, he recorded that while the male produces a hoarse bellow which can be heard a hundred metres away, 'the female never uses her voice'. The eggs were white and spherical, and 'one which I measured was seven inches and three eighths in circumference and therefore larger than a hen's egg'. Where the soil was sufficiently loose, the female would deposit her eggs together and cover them up with sand. He was told that when the young were hatched, they would be killed in great numbers by the buzzards.

Darwin had become an incomparable observer himself but he also knew how to benefit from other people's knowledge. An outstanding example of this was when he learned from Lawson that he could tell by one look which island any particular tortoise came from. It was mainly a question of the shape of their shells, tortoises which had to stretch upwards for their food having an arched elevation at the front of their shells, while those which fed on cactus nearer the ground had shells which were concave all round. Thus, the tortoises of Albemarle Island (in fact, there was a distinct race on each of the Albemarle volcanoes) had developed a different-shaped shell from those on Chatham, and both were different from those on Charles' or James'. At the time this fact made relatively little impact on Darwin's mind, but it was stored away and germinated later.

Darwin carefully collected twenty-six species of land birds on James' Island alone but was at first glance less impressed with these than with the other fauna or the flora, their colours being nothing like as striking as those of most other tropical birds. Only later did he find that the birds gave particularly significant clues in the scientific treasure hunt on which he had embarked. What most intrigued him about the birds was their tameness, the point which had struck earlier visitors. One day a mockingbird perched to drink on a pitcher of water (made of a tortoise shell) which Darwin was carrying in his hand. 'A gun,' he said, 'is here almost superfluous; for with the muzzle of one I pushed a hawk off the branch of a tree.' In *The Voyage of a Naturalist Round the World* he quoted Cowley's and Dampier's descriptions from the buccaneering visits, which showed that the birds were then even tamer, but points out that even 150 years of persecution by man had not made the birds wild.

On Charles' Island, which had been permanently colonised for some years in 1835, Darwin saw a boy 'sitting by a well with a switch in his hand, with which he killed the doves and finches as they came to drink. He had already procured a little heap of them for his dinner, and he said he had constantly been in the habit of waiting there for the same purpose'. It is the extraordinary tameness of the birds and other animals, even today, which gives the Galapagos environment its magical, Arcadian atmosphere. How much more this must have struck Darwin and his companions!

The collections which Darwin made during his short stay, and the notes and impressions which he brought away, gave him food for thought for the rest of the *Beagle's* voyage and for most of the rest of his life. They contained the seeds which produced a revolution in human thought of which we can still feel the reverberations today. But all this was in the future when HMS *Beagle* sailed from the Galapagos on October20th, 1835 towards Tahiti.

When she had arrived five weeks before, FitzRoy, Darwin and everyone else on board thought they were entering something resembling hell itself, and were repelled by the barren, lava-strewn shores. Not even Darwin, who saw most of the islands, could find much to say in praise of the landscapes, even in the greener and damper interiors of the islands. However, all who were able to spend time ashore felt the awesome timelessness and the innocence of the natural world they found there.

11

The Origin of Species

CHARLES DARWIN LEFT ENGLAND in 1831 with a firm belief in Christian teaching about the creation as it is explained in the Book of Genesis. It was not until 1837 that he clearly recorded the beginning of his conversion to the belief that life was created not by a single exercise of divine power but by the infinitely slow process of evolution. In that year he started a notebook entitled *Transmutation of Species* in which he wrote: 'Had been greatly struck from about month of previous March on character of South American fossils and species on Galapagos Archipelago. These facts origin (especially latter) of all my views.' Some years later he wrote a description in the 1845 edition of his journal, which, by its emphasis and grandeur, leaves no doubt of the deep impression which the Galapagos experience had on him.

> The natural history of these islands is eminently curious and well deserves attention. Most of the organic productions are aboriginal creatures, found nowhere else; there is even a difference between the inhabitants of the different islands; yet all show a marked relationship with those of America ... The archipelago is a little world within itself, or rather a satellite attached to America ... considering the small size of these islands, we feel the more astonished at the number of their

aboriginal beings, and at their confined range . . . Hence, both in space and time, we seem to be brought somewhat near to that great fact, that mystery of mysteries, the first appearance of new beings on this earth.

This was written nine years after the end of the voyage of the *Beagle*, and Darwin was to spend another fourteen years working out and demonstrating, with a mass of detailed research, the laws and mechanisms which produced new species by evolution.

The route which Darwin followed to reach this point of departure was provided by geology. While the biology of the Galapagos may have produced the fire, the geology of the South American continent was the tinderbox, and the spark was the new thinking expounded by Charles Lyell in his *Principles of Geology*, which worked in Darwin's mind in the long months of the *Beagle's* voyage. Lyell's book pointed to a totally new explanation for the palaeontological evidence which he observed in rock strata and fossil remains. Ingenious theories had been devised by scholars, such as Cuvier, to reconcile the Bible's assertion of a divine creation of the Earth with the fact that some animal and plant species had evidently become extinct in remote times. Lyell argued that the Earth's creation and growth had been a process occupying many millions of years. His views were in flat contradiction of the ecclesiastical theory (reached by an extraordinary series of calculations made by Archbishop Ussher and Dr John Lightfoot) that the world was created on Sunday October 23rd in the year 4004BC. Lyell said nothing about the evolution of life on Earth, but he showed that the Earth itself had been formed by elevation and subsidence of the crust, and by erosion and the effects of climate over almost limitless periods of time. This concept of change coming about with unimaginable slowness over millennia was to prove a turning point in scientific thought.

Even before he reached the Galapagos Darwin, while still holding firmly to the conventional Christian teaching, was finding evidence to bear out Lyell's views. In Patagonia he discovered an ossuary – 'a perfect catacomb' – of the bones of extinct mammals. To his great surprise he found fossil relics of some animals whose structures were very like those of the animals he now saw around him on the pampas. Fossils were time indicators of geological progression. They were also incontrovertible evidence that some of the living species to be observed in South America in 1834 had evolved from similar prehistoric forms of life. It seemed from this evidence that some species had become extinct many, many years before the alleged date of the creation of the world, while others had evolved into different forms over similar very long periods of time.

Darwin's next opportunity to study geological change was a memorable occasion in Chile. Caught in a major earthquake on the coast, he saw with his own eyes how the level of the land could be raised or lowered by seismic cataclysm. He made long expeditions into the Andes (including one right across them and down as far as Mendoza in Argentina), on which he saw fossil shells of creatures which were once crawling on the bottom of the sea now standing nearly 4,200 metres above sea-level. FitzRoy, reflecting the proper Biblical view of the matter, argued that the shells had been deposited at 4,200 metres by the Flood. However, Darwin now felt that it was far more likely that they had come there as the result of a slow elevation of the land itself over eons of time.

It was in the Galapagos, as a result of the biological evidence which he found there, that Darwin first began to extend Lyell's thinking outside the geological field. As he began to study and speculate about the specimens he had collected during the remainder of the *Beagle*'s voyage (and it was nearly a year before she docked finally at Falmouth), Darwin's thoughts began to move in parallel to Lyell's. While still in the islands he had noted in his diary for September 26th: 'It will be very interesting to find from future comparison to what district or "centre of creation" the organised beings of this archipelago must be attached.' Consciously or not, Darwin seems to be wondering whether the creatures around him had appeared in the form he saw, divinely created, or whether they had developed from an immigrant root in response to the particular conditions in the islands. Mulling over his specimens, he was struck by an intriguing fact. The majority of them were unique species or races found in the Galapagos Islands and nowhere else. According to the creationist view these species should be identical to those found in other archipelagos with similar conditions, but they were not. Darwin could see when he studied the plant, reptile, bird or fish specimens that they resembled much more closely the corresponding species existing in South America, while differing from them in some obvious ways. He realised, too, that the variations Lawson had pointed out between the species found on different islands applied not only to the tortoises but also to the mockingbirds, various plants and to the finches. Some islands had several of their own distinct species.

The finches, on first acquaintance, had seemed rather uninteresting: they all had short tails, the same colouring, built similar nests and laid white eggs spotted with pink. Darwin found, however, that they had certain peculiar differences and that there were no fewer than thirteen different species, and 'the most curious fact is the perfect graduation in the size of the beaks of the different species'. One island had finches with strong, thick beaks for cracking nuts or seeds; another race had beaks shaped for catching insects; in a third the beak was adapted for feeding on fruit or flowers. There was even a species which had learned to use a twig to dig out grubs from their holes.

When he published the first version of his journal in 1839 he had little to say about the finches. However, in 1845 he prepared the revised edition, which shows that he now felt sure of the logic of his evidence: 'Seeing this gradation and diversity of structure in one small intimately-related group of birds, one might really fancy that from an original paucity of birds in the archipelago, one species had been taken and modified for different ends.' This put into words, albeit as a hypothesis, a revolutionary idea which contradicted all the accepted theories about the origin of life and the divine creation of immutable species. He had yet to explain how the modification and evolution of species could actually happen. If they had not arrived in the Galapagos by divine intervention, how had they come? Having seen in Chile that the land could be forced up out of the sea, Darwin assumed that the Galapagos had also been created in this way. The majority of geologists still agree with this view. At first there was no life at all on the smoking craters and lava flows, but cooling and weathering processes over millions of years would form pockets of soil, and seeds brought from the mainland by the wind or by birds would produce primitive vegetation. Other seeds and animal life would arrive on floating logs or the huge masses of vegetation which even now drift great distances from the American river estuaries. The current which brought Bishop Berlanga from the mainland could bring much else, and the bigger creatures may have arrived in this way or, in the case of tortoises, for example, they may have been aquatic originally and later developed into land animals.

He thus had an explanation of how life had reached the Galapagos in the first place. It was not easy to believe, but was not so incredible (for him) as attributing it all to divine intervention. Now he had to explain how the various Galapagos species evolved from their common, continental progenitor.

In 1838 Charles Darwin, like other serious Victorian gentlemen and scholars, read Malthus' *Essay on Population*. He tells us in his autobiography that he read Malthus 'for amusement', but it had an outcome crucial for Darwin's own work. Malthus argued that human population would increase at a geometrical rate it if were not for the harsh limitation imposed by the far slower rate of growth of the means of subsistence, the food supply. Darwin saw that this principle could be applied equally to the whole of natural creation. Each species that had arrived on the Galapagos had either adjusted itself to the available food supply or perished. All living things had been submitted to the same test and those which survived, including man, were the ones who were more adaptable, more skilful or more aggressive than their competitors.

It had long been known that small random variations did sometimes occur in nature. Breeders of plants and animals had learned to use random variations which were advantageous as the basis for improving their stocks. Given the law that Malthus had propounded, it followed that the animal or plant which had the benefit of a small advantageous variation would have a better chance of survival than others, and if the variation was inheritable, it would be passed on to the next generation. Similarly a disadvantageous variation would reduce the chances of survival. Where such a random change occurred, for example in the size or shape of a bird's bill, it might enable the bird to exploit a new source of food and encourage it to multiply. If the change were unfavourable the result would be the elimination of birds with that particular variation. Over the millennia in which Darwin now knew that nature worked, this process of 'natural selection' could produce similar results to those deliberately produced by horses or rose breeders in infinitely less time.

It was, yet again, the birds (known ever since as Darwin's finches) which illustrated this theory most clearly and beautifully. The original immigrant finches had unprecedented scope for modification because there was so little competition on the islands they came to inhabit. Had there already been other types of birds – warblers, tits, woodpeckers and so on – on the islands, finches which changed by random mutation so as to compete with these birds would probably not have survived alongside the established species. For example, finches which evolved woodpecker-like characteristics would not have flourished in an area where there were efficient woodpeckers already filling that ecological niche. However, with no woodpeckers established in the Galapagos, the finch was free to develop into a 'woodpecker-finch' and exploit that niche, and in time a new species had evolved.

In 1842 Darwin for the first time drafted a summary of his

theory in thirty-five pages. Two years later he expanded this to two hundred and thirty pages, and then in 1845, as we have seen, he brought himself to publish piecemeal some comments which showed the world at large how his mind was working and what conclusions must be drawn. By then he had had the benefit of specialist assessments of his Galapagos and other specimens from Lyell (geology), Gould (ornithology) and Hooker (botany). There was really nothing to prevent him publishing his theory in a fully-considered form. Yet it took another fourteen years before he could bring himself to do so.

The slow and painstaking development of his theory led Darwin ultimately to the proposition that man had evolved from a creature more primitive even than the apes of modern times. This was regarded as the most blasphemous outrage of all when he finally published *On the Origin of Species by Natural Selection* in 1859. Not only the ecclesiastical authorities and all Christian believers, but the vast majority of the human race, if asked, would certainly have preferred the idea of being made in the image of God to Darwin's proposition that they had descended or evolved from ape-like creatures.

Darwin was aware that he was exploring totally new territory which would clearly arouse bitter opposition, and that he risked ridicule if he could not support his theory at every point with a mass of evidence. Perhaps he was also discouraged by finding that even close collaborators, like Lyell and Hooker, did not seem to agree with him about the principle and significance of natural selection. Few, if any, contemporary scientists doubted the permanence of species.

However, Darwin's basic reluctance came from his own character. He knew that his theory would be deeply shocking to the public, to the Church and to most scholars. Certainly he dreaded the reaction of his wife, who was deeply religious, and, in a sense, his views were unpalatable to himself. He had ceased to believe in Christianity as a divine revelation years before, but he was never willing, if he could help it, to lend any support to those who wished to attack religion frontally. He knew what a storm these heretical ideas would raise, and although he knew he was right, he may sometimes have wished he was not. He wrote to his friend Hooker in 1844: 'At last gleams of light have come, and I am almost convinced (quite contrary to the opinion I started with) that species are not (it is like confessing a murder) immutable.'

In 1858, the 'murder' finally came out. A younger naturalist, Alfred Russel Wallace, who had worked for many years in the Amazon jungle and then in Malaya, sent Darwin an essay entitled *On the Tendencies of Varieties to Depart Indefinitely from the Original Type*. This essay, although it was not supported by the mass of evidence which Darwin had put together over the previous twenty-five years, came to exactly the same conclusion. In February 1858 Wallace was suffering an attack of fever in the Molucca Islands when he recalled the book by Malthus on population and asked himself:

> Why do some die and some live? And the answer was clearly that on the whole the best fitted lived. The more I thought over it, the more I became convinced that I had at length found the long-sought-for law of nature that solved the problem of the Origin of Species, and I wrote it out carefully in order to send it to Darwin by the next post.

It duly arrived on Darwin's desk at Down House in Kent, where he noted the same day: 'I never saw a more striking coincidence; if Wallace had my M/S sketch written out in 1842 he could not have made a better short abstract.'

Darwin was thus faced with the prospect that all his work would be in vain, but he behaved admirably and forwarded the essay to Lyell. Happily, both Lyell and Hooker insisted that Darwin should not step aside, and persuaded him to let Wallace's paper and one of his own be read to the Linnean Society in London straight away.

The next year he published *On the Origin of Species by Means of Natural Selection, or the Preservation of Favoured Races in the Struggle for life*. It was an instant best-seller. The first edition of one thousand two hundred and fifty copies sold out on the day of publication and it led to perhaps the greatest intellectual row of the nineteenth century.

Some scientists, even some with deep religious convictions, had already moved a long way towards accepting a theory of evolution in principle. Darwin noted that at least thirty-four authors writing before 1859 believed in the modification of species. However, the theory was bitterly opposed by many scientists and, even more so, by the Church and its hierarchy. At the famous Oxford meeting of the British Association in 1860 Darwin's champions, led by Hooker and T. H. Huxley, were faced by the mid-Victorian clergy, with all their awesome authority, led by the Bishop of Oxford, Samuel Wilberforce, otherwise known as 'Soapy Sam'. At the time of this great debate neither side convinced the other, but when the dust settled, it could be seen that the weight of evidence produced by Darwin had decisively changed the scientists' and eventually the laymen's view of the world. Gradually it was recognised that the living world was a world in movement, that life was subject to constant change and evolution.

On the Origin of Species, which literally changed our view of the world and of our own destiny, was begun when Darwin set sail in the *Beagle* and, in particular, when he found himself in the 'living laboratory of evolution' – the Galapagos archipelago. Had he not been there, he or someone else would eventually have reached the same conclusion, but by a different and longer route. The Galapagos stimulated thoughts about the origin of things and made men ask themselves fundamental questions which did not seem to arise with the same sharpness elsewhere.

Darwin was not the first visitor to be provoked into speculation by what he saw. In 1709 the privateer Captain Woodes Rogers, who claimed to be concerned with naval tactics and commercial profit, leaving natural philosophy to others, found himself forced into speculation: 'There are guanas in abundance and land turtles almost on every island. 'Tis strange how they got here because they can't come of themselves, and none of that sort are to be found on the Main.' A century later, David Porter, who also had plenty of other problems to worry about, put the question even more directly:

I shall leave others to account for the manner in which all those islands obtained their supply of tortoises and guanas and other animals of the reptile kind; it is not my business even to conjecture as to the cause. I shall merely state that those islands have every appearance of having been newly created, and that those are perhaps the only part of the animal creation that could subsist on them... Nature has created them elsewhere and why could she not do it as well on those islands?

The fact that these questions occurred to others before Darwin is confirmation that those almost empty heaps of lava in the Pacific contain evidence of evolution in forms which are easier for men to understand than anywhere else. It was Darwin's genius to combine powers of observation as acute as any of his forerunners, a mind free from the rigidity that comes from orthodox training, fabulous industry, intellectual integrity, and the single-minded concentration to devote his whole adult life to following through the first insights and inspiration which came to him at the age of twenty-six in the Galapagos.

12

Colonial Ambitions

AFTER 1832 THE GOVERNMENT of Ecuador had a theoretical responsibility for events in the Galapagos. However, this young republic, struggling to maintain itself in its early years against threats of violent revolution, anarchy and every kind of domestic stress on the mainland, had no means of controlling events on the islands, and usually did not even know the situation there. The most they could do was appoint a responsible person, such as General Villamil, to administer the settlement and try to control the activities of any foreigners who arrived. Had Captain David Porter succeeded in annexing the archipelago for the United States in 1812 (a proposal which horrified his superiors in Washington and for which they reprimanded him) the United States Government would certainly have done no more. Britain and other European countries of the time were equally lax about providing some kind of decent government in the remote territories and islands which they were busily acquiring in that expansive age of colonisation.

As we have seen, when FitzRoy and Darwin arrived in 1835 they found a population of between two and three hundred people who were able to sustain themselves tolerably well by cultivating crops on the higher moist zone, and hunting wild pigs and goats when they wanted a change from the traditional Galapagos diet of tortoise meat. Villamil kept the colony going for five years, but never seems to have made much progress in establishing the orchilla moss industry – the economic reason for settling the island in the first place. In 1837 Villamil gave up and returned to the mainland. He was replaced as governor by Colonel José Williams (an Ecuadorian officer who presumably had English or North American forebears), and General Mena took over the management of the colonising enterprise.

Even before Villamil left, the constant arrival of criminals from the mainland had turned the colony into little more than a penal settlement. He had acquired a pack of dogs which moved about with him everywhere to protect him from the violence of his 'subjects', and the island became known as the Dog Kingdom. Williams was a cruel overseer, intent only on using convict labour for his own profit, and things went from bad to worse. The tortoise population became extinct on Charles' Island at about this time and, for this or other reasons, the population scattered over several islands. In 1841 those who remained on Charles' rose in revolt against the brutal Williams, and he fled for his life. When Villamil eventually returned to see how much of his investment could be saved from the wreck, he found only a few dozen convicts left, living in squalid penury on Charles'. By 1852 the settlement which Villamil had originally named 'The Haven of Peace' was finally abandoned and, perhaps for the first time, justified its name. In the same year the Swedish frigate *Eugenie*, visiting the archipelago for scientific purposes, found and rescued a shipwrecked American sailor, who was the last man left alive on Charles' Island. Perhaps the only surprise about this first attempt to settle the islands is that it lasted as long as it did. Villamil removed such assets as he could to Chatham Island where, with the help of General Mena he hoped to make a fresh start. His idea was to mine coal, but since the island is volcanic this failed too.

There was a dramatic postscript to the story of Villamil's settlement, which like so much of the earlier history of the Galapagos, involves piracy and violent death. In 1851 some of the convicts who had been moved from Charles' to Chatham stole a boat there, returned in it to Charles', and contrived to capture an American whaler, the *George Howland*, by ambushing her crew while they were ashore looking for water. The convicts planned to go in for piracy and privateering with an audacity which even the city of Guayaquil and the Guayas river settlements had never experienced before. They were led by a man named Briones, who earned himself the nickname 'the Pirate of Guayas'. He had got wind of a *coup d'état* being planned in Peru by General Juan José Flores, who had been the first president of Ecuador and wished to seize power once more. Briones conceived the bold scheme of intervening in this affair on the side of the established government, thereby, as he hoped, earning a pardon for himself and his companions, as well as any booty which fell into their hands.

Their first step was to settle accounts with General Mena, and they forced the remainder of the American whaler's crew at knife point to sail the ship back to Chatham Island, which had become the official 'capital'. Arriving there in the guise of an innocent whaler, the convicts brought off a surprise attack. General Mena and Captain Barroterán were promptly murdered, and Briones and company set sail for the mainland in the *George Howland* with the pick of the stores.

General Flores armed a group of his supporters and set out to invade Guayaquil in five small boats, a plan which was likely to succeed only if executed with the benefit of total surprise. We shall never know whether it would have worked, but the General's security was obviously very poor. Briones, despite having come direct from Galapagos where any news took weeks or months to penetrate, succeeded in intercepting the sloop which formed the vanguard of this mini-armada, boarded it and killed the crew of twenty-nine Flores supporters. With this victory behind him, Briones sailed into Guayaquil expecting to be received as the hero who had rescued his country from a violent revolution. Perhaps the Guayaquil authorities were inclined to Flores, or perhaps they remembered too well how much their city had suffered in the past from pirates. Whatever the reason, they failed to live up to Briones' hopes. He and his band of convict-pirates were seized, tried and hanged for the murders they had committed.

The capture of the American whaler *George Howland*, and Briones' short career as a latter-day pirate, led to international repercussions and put the Galapagos for the first time on the political map. The United States chargé d'affaires in Quito, Courtland Cushing, slapped in a claim for forty thousand US dollars against the Republic of Ecuador as compensation to the owners and crew of the ship. He also pointed out to Washington that since the government in Quito had little interest in making its authority felt in the Galapagos, and that the main users were United States' vessels, this might be a good moment for Washington to consider acquiring the islands. United States governments were not immune from the ambition, which all European countries cheerfully indulged, to collect colonial territories, strategic outposts and, failing all else, privileged commercial positions wherever they could be found round the world. Courtland Cushing may have been a little unrealistic, but he was obviously a man of his time.

There was no particularly strong economic, or as yet strategic, reason for the United States to wish to assume control of the Galapagos. However, before long a motive was produced by none other than General Villamil. Undaunted by repeated failures to capitalise on the rich resources which he was sure existed, the General persuaded friends in the United States that the islands contained large deposits of guano. Cushing apparently believed this too, and when General Villamil was appointed Ecuadorian chargé d'affaires in Washington in 1853 negotiations began to quicken. The only other convenient source of guano for the United States at that time were deposits on which Peru had a monopoly, and which she naturally exploited for the highest price she could get.

A number of offers to work the guano in the Galapagos, with or without a transfer of sovereignty, were put forward and considered in Ecuador. A convention was signed in 1854 which, in return for a loan of three million dollars, gave the United States rights to acquire the guano, and conceded certain special privileges to its citizens involved in the business, but affirmed Ecuadorian sovereignty over the islands. The moving spirit behind the agreement was, of course, General Villamil in partnership with aspiring entrepreneurs in the United States. Sadly, it proved yet again that the General's faith in the richness of the Galapagos had run ahead of the facts. Deeper and less partial study showed that there were no guano deposits. When this became known, American interest evaporated; the convention was not ratified by the Senate, and the Ecuadorian government nullified it in 1855.

Meanwhile the proposed convention had produced angry reactions from a number of other governments. Spain, France, Peru and Britain all protested against what they saw as unacceptable privileges being granted to the United States to the detriment of their own political and commercial interests. This protest had no sound basis, for Ecuador had every right to dispose of the archipelago and its assets in any way it wished. Nevertheless, a fine storm broke out in the diplomatic teacups.

The leading spirit among the protesters seems to have been France, at that time governed by the Emperor Napoleon III and imbued with ideas of establishing French hegemony over the whole of Mexico and Latin America. France contrived to persuade yet another country, Chile, to join in the opposition to the convention. The furore caused by this misconceived agreement subsided as quickly as it arose, but the alienation of the Galapagos continued to preoccupy maritime countries for many years afterwards and it was to prove one of the most delicate matters which Ecuadorian governments had to handle.

Transfer of sovereignty over the Galapagos to another country had, in fact, been discussed previously. In 1851, there was a proposal to hand the islands over to British private ownership in settlement of a loan which had been floated in London at the time of the wars of liberation. The bond-holders in Britain saw little prospect of the loan being repaid in cash, and were unwise enough to consider accepting titles to land in the Galapagos instead. This proposal was dropped partly because Ecuador came under contrary pressure from Peru and – perhaps more probably – because discharging a thirty-year-old debt was a less attractive proposition than acquiring a new loan of three million dollars.

On another occasion there seems to have been an offer of the islands to France. Underlying these episodes was the simple fact that none of the countries with political or commercial interests on the Pacific coast of South America had strong enough motives to make them press seriously for direct control of the islands, but all of them were determined not to allow any rival power to control the archipelago. The British, for example, knew that an unfriendly naval force in the Galapagos such as the single ship commanded by Captain David Porter in 1812 could do very serious damage to shipping. The United States fiercely resisted any move on the part of Britain, or another European power, to gain control of the islands. Peru and Chile, the two South American states with the largest ambitions in the Pacific, were already fiercely jealous of one another and eventually joined issue in the Pacific War of 1878. Neither would tolerate the other having any kind of foothold in the Galapagos. So the Galapagos had only a negative strategic importance.

No valuable resources had yet been discovered in the islands in significant quantity; they were not conveniently placed for the normal shipping routes; and they were not suitable for settlement on any large scale. Despite this, any wise government in Quito was keen to turn Ecuadorian property to advantage by finding a government for whom the Galapagos held some special attraction. At the same time no government in Ecuador could countenance any scheme which might involve compromising the national honour or sovereignty over the archipelago. This was to commit political suicide, as a succession of presidents were to discover. Trumping up a charge of intending to give away the nation's sovereignty over the islands, whatever the inducement, became a strong and convenient stick with which to attack political opponents.

However, concern for their fate stopped here, for the rest of the country was deeply split. The people of the coastal plains centred on Guayaquil lived by the cultivation of tropical crops such as sugar, bananas, coffee and cocoa, and by trade and commerce. The totally different Indian population of the high Andes were limited to subsistence farming in their mountain valleys and the majority of them still lived under a form of serfdom introduced at the time of the Spanish conquest. Neither of these populations knew much about each other, let alone the handful of convicts or political undesirables who were trying to scratch some kind of living among the lava flows of the Galapagos. Even the ruling elites – the merchants of Guayaquil and the landed families of the high sierras – had little more knowledge of the islands and no great interest in the welfare of their inhabitants. Governments of this young and cruelly poor republic had to fight for their very survival, and were usually replaced by coup d'état or revolution, if not submerged by anarchy. Preoccupied with preserving themselves and keeping chaos at arm's length, no Ecuadorian government could provide proper administration in the Galapagos. In harsh reality there was no hope that law and order could be maintained there, or human life protected by outside authority.

These were the conditions when the next efforts were made to settle and develop the Galapagos Islands. In 1858 Manuel Cobos and José Monroy formed the Orchillera Company on Chatham Island to exploit the orchilla moss which festooned much of the vegetation in the Galapagos. It had already become a significant export of the mainland province of Manabí, and should have offered worthwhile possibilities for the islands. However, as before, the business did not prosper and the company's concession to gather and export orchilla was taken over in 1870 by another optimist from the mainland, José de Valdizán. He moved to Charles'

Island, and for some years made progress by reviving the Haven of Peace settlement left by General Villamil. Then, in 1878, the tragedy of 1841 was disastrously repeated when a group of Valdizán's workers seized some arms and went on the rampage. The revolt turned into a pitched battle between mutineers and the law-abiding remainder of the settlement. Valdizán was murdered together with many others, including all but one of the mutineers, his colony collapsed and the remaining settlers scattered to other islands.

Cobos had built up another settlement, on Chatham Island, which he hopefully christened 'El Progreso'. After the murder of Valdizán he left the islands for ten years, but eventually ventured back with a new group of a hundred convict workers, and a good deal more capital to revive the enterprise. He planted sugar cane on a large scale, built a sugar mill and a wharf, and established market gardens and orchards. El Progreso began to live up to its name, and in some ways it flourished more than any of its predecessors. However, Cobos, free of any restraining authority in his remote island, was developing the economy of the settlement on a basis little different from slavery. He paid wages in a token currency which could only be spent in his own shop and, since he owned the only ship serving the island, he was able to prevent workers leaving without his permission. The central government eventually appointed an administrator but he was evidently in Cobos's pocket, and had no control over the mounting abuses and tyranny. Inevitably in an environment where there was no law but force, the episode had a bloody and violent ending. In 1904 a sloop with no ship's papers arrived in Colombia carrying seventy-seven men and eight women. Slowly their story came out and it shocked the country.

Cobos had apparently been murdered by one of his 'workers'. The whole settlement had thereupon seized the ship and abandoned the island, since they saw no other possible escape from what amounted to imprisonment with hard labour for life. At their trial the prisoners made the most horrible charges against their former master: appallingly savage punishments were habitual at El Progreso; six men had been flogged to death; others who had fallen foul of Cobos had been marooned on waterless islands; Cobos' body had been buried on the spot where he had executed five other men. There was no corroboration of these stories, and so the government, stung into action, sent a gunboat, the *Cotopaxi*, to investigate. This found enough evidence to prove that Cobos had been responsible for savage ill-treatment of his prisoners. One of the men he had marooned was found on the beach of Santa Cruz, where he had managed to survive for three years. He had kept count of time by cutting notches on trees and barely sustained life on raw turtles and iguanas, using cactus pads in place of water. He had been unable to reach other parts of the island through the murderous undergrowth. The final tragedy was that this man might have been rescued by passing ships if Cobos had not placed a notice for them to see which said, both in Spanish and English: 'Do not take this man away. He is twenty times a criminal'. Another man marooned on James' Island was never found alive. Some years later his skeleton was discovered by a visiting American scientific expedition.

In 1893 another unsuccessful attempt to colonise Charles' Island was made by Antonio Gil. After four years he abandoned it in favour of Albemarle, where he eventually established two settlements, one called Villamil on the south-east coast, and the main centre of Santo Tomás inland on the lower slopes of the largest crater on the island. In 1905 there were almost two hundred people on Albemarle getting some sort of living by exporting sulphur and lime to the mainland. Their margin of survival was slim because they continued to depend for drinking water on a few water-holes near the shore.

These stories – and there must be many similar unrecorded incidents – show the Galapagos archipelago as a sinister backdrop against which all human dramas are doomed to tragedy. There seems to be something inimical to human life or at least to human happiness in the very atmosphere. In the opening pages of his book

The Encantadas, Herman Melville described the impression which the islands produced on him when he came there in the whaler *Acushnet* in the 1840s:

> It is to be doubted whether any spot on earth can in desolateness furnish a parallel to this group. Abandoned cemeteries of long ago, old cities by piecemeal tumbling to their ruin, these are melancholy enough; but like all else which had but once been associated with humanity, they still awaken some thoughts of sympathy, however sad... But the special curse, as one may call it, of the Encantadas, that which exalts them in desolation above Idumea and the Pole, is that to them change never comes; neither the change of season, nor of sorrows. Cut by the Equator, they know not autumn and they know not spring; while already reduced to the lees of fire, ruin itself can work little more upon them... Another feature in these isles is their emphatic uninhabitableness. It is deemed a fit type of all-forsaken overthrow, that the jackal itself should den in the wastes of weedy Babylon; but the Encantadas refuse to harbour even the outcasts of the beasts. Man and wolf alike disown them. Little but reptile life is here found; tortoises, lizards, immense spiders, snakes and that strangest anomaly of outlandish nature, the iguano. No voice, no low, no howl is heard; the chief sound of life here is a hiss.

Melville did not believe in understatement and his zoology is erratic, but he saw more clearly than anyone that the Galapagos were not fit for men. The repeated efforts to establish settlements in the nineteenth century produced almost no benefit for their promoters. For the convict and other workers who were forced to wrench some sort of existence from the lava slopes, the only returns for their efforts were, at best, a harsh life and an early death. However, one breed adapted itself enthusiastically and happily to the Galapagos and flourished: the scientist.

13

Scientists and Castaways

AFTER DARWIN CAME THE FLOOD. With the long Victorian peace, the navies of the world were free to indulge themselves in cruises of discovery in remote parts of the oceans, and their voyages in the Pacific concentrated more and more on scientific enquiry. One of the most remarkable pieces of scientific work achieved in the Galapagos was the hydrographic work of Robert FitzRoy, which has been unduly overshadowed by Darwin's more startling achievements. FitzRoy's charts made navigation in the archipelago a far less difficult and dangerous undertaking for all those, including successive generations of scientists, who came after him. The captain of the French ship *La Génie*, which followed in 1846 with the same primary task as FitzRoy of charting the archipelago, gave glowing praise for the latter's work:

> Nothing escaped the perspicacity of this conscientious observer; the smallest details are all indicated with really astonishing precision and following his drawing one can visualize in the most accurate manner the shape of the coast. Coming after him there is not even an opportunity to glean.

Even more to FitzRoy's credit is the verdict of the American scientist, J. R. Slevin, who wrote in 1959:

It is truly amazing that the modern chart of the Galapagos made in 1942 by the USS *Bowditch* . . . equipped with every modern device should so closely approximate the survey made by Captain FitzRoy over a hundred years ago. His little vessel was at the mercy of strong and uncertain currents, together with deadly calms so prevalent in those regions.

Since Ambrose Cowley, the buccaneer, and Captain Colnett had been responsible for the only reliable (or least unreliable) charts in their time, British mariners had made a dominant contribution to the exploration of the Galapagos and their scientific study. For a century after Colnett's visit Britain was the leading maritime power in the world, and it would be tedious to enumerate the British men-of-war which visited Galapagos in the nineteenth century. Thus it was no accident that an English naturalist, Darwin, had been first in the field in the Galapagos.

However, once scientific minds focused on these remote islands other nationalities joined in. One of the first organised expeditions was an American one led by Professor Louis Agassiz of Harvard University, in the USS *Hassler* in 1872. He was very quickly followed by the outstanding German scholar, Dr Theodor Wolf, who, while living and teaching in Quito, was encouraged by the Ecuadorian government to make two protracted expeditions to study the geology and other aspects of the islands. There were many others, but the relative proximity of the United States and its growing weight, in scholarship as in other ways, meant that American scientists came to the Galapagos more often than Europeans.

The scientists were bound to plunge into dissent – the inevitable result of their search for deeper and wider knowledge – and this happened immediately among the geologists. Professor George Baur, arriving in 1891 from Clark University, quickly decided that the islands were the peaks of a larger land mass once linked to the South American continent, which had subsided. As we have already seen in Chapter 3, this theory has important implications for zoologists and botanists as well as geologists. Baur was supported by a number of other scientists who followed him such as Ridgway, Gadow and van Denburgh. This subsidence school was categorically opposed by others, including Wolf, Wallace and Agassiz. Darwin had been one of the first to advance the view that the islands had been formed by separate volcanic thrust from the seabed and that their origin was therefore oceanic. The war between supporters of these theories continues to this day, with the majority of opinion on the side of the oceanic school.

The other striking feature of most scientific exploration in the Galapagos, during this great era of exploration, study and colonisation was perhaps less admirable. The settlers were killing for food to eat or to sell to visiting ships, and the scientists were adding to the general depredation. It is possible to understand and even excuse the slaughter of tortoises by those who needed fresh meat to keep alive and free from disease. Many had good reason for taking advantage of an obvious source of food in a hard world where even bare necessities were scarce. There is less excuse for the scientists who, in their ignorance or stupidity, took many hundred of tortoises for their collections, and continued doing so until as recently as the 1930s.

An analysis of expedition reports published in 1914 by John van Denburgh showed that at least five hundred tortoises had been taken up to that time. The New York Zoological Society took as many as one hundred and eighty in 1928. In his book *Darwin's Islands: A Natural History of the Galapagos*, Ian Thornton tells us how scientists, after collecting on an island, would declare the tortoise extinct there only for some later expedition to discover and remove the survivors, once again claiming them as specimens of a 'dying' race. Thornton points out that these 'last survivors were collected from Duncan by four different expeditions in 1897, 1898, 1900 and 1901, and yet the *Academy* expedition of 1905–6 discovered eighty-six tortoises on that island, which they killed and removed for study; over sixty of these were females.'

Making every allowance for the differing perceptions and attitudes towards the natural world which prevailed at the beginning of the 20th century, it is hard to believe that these people were moved only by altruistic and scientific motives. In many cases, if not all, they appear little better than eager schoolboys collecting birds' eggs. However, their actions were considered legitimate by all concerned, for it was the received wisdom of that time that the best place to study natural history was in laboratories or museums.

This certainly seems to have been the view of Rollo Beck, perhaps the most distinguished of the American scientists to lead early expeditions to the Galapagos. He was sponsored by a wealthy amateur collector, Lord Rothschild, on expeditions in 1897 and 1901, which returned with large numbers of living tortoises for Rothschild's private collection in England. Subsequently, Beck was chosen as the leader of the California Academy of Sciences expedition which was the largest and most elaborate collecting expedition ever to reach the Galapagos.

In the converted schooner, the *Academy*, Beck arrived in the islands on September 24th, 1905, at the head of an integrated team including specialists in geology, entomology, ornithology, zoology, botany and herpetology. They spent a complete year in systematic study of the ecology of each of the islands in turn, and in the collection of specimens. The historian of the expedition, J. R. Slevin, claims that they 'brought back by far the largest collections of birds, mammals, reptiles, insects and plants that have ever been taken' and there is no reason to doubt him. They collected, for example, no less than eigth thousand six hundred and ninety-one specimens of birds and two hundred and sixty-six giant tortoises, including examples of all fifteen species then surviving and skeletons of those which had become extinct. These massive collections formed the raw material for an enormous volume of work which was produced in subsequent years by each of the scientists and by other specialists at the California Academy and elsewhere. For example, Harry S. Swarth and E. W. Gifford produced works on the birds; Allan

Stewart on the flora; Francis Williams on the butterflies and moths; and John van Denburgh on the reptiles.

The justification for taking away such enormous numbers of specimens from the islands for study in California is summed up in the view which Rollo Beck formed when he first visited the Galapagos. He concluded that the tortoises, which were his speciality, were in danger of extinction throughout the archipelago because the existing stocks were still being killed off for their oil (which could be sold in Guayaquil for a dollar a gallon) while the young were being killed by predators such as the wild dogs and the rats. Beck calculated that not more than one in ten thousand tortoises hatched, escaped being killed off in this way soon after birth, and he believed that the seals and the iguanas were likely to suffer the same fate and also become extinct in relatively few years. He felt (too pessimistically, as we now know) that these species were unlikely to survive unless protected, and realised that there was no possibility of any form of protection being forthcoming. Even if it had occurred to governments of that time to protect wildlife, there would have been no means of doing so in this remote group of islands. If the alternative was extermination, Beck and his team felt that it was better that the wildlife should be killed and taken away for study. As late as 1928 it was thought that the tortoise would become extinct, and another American expedition took a considerable number back to the States for distribution there in the hope that they would at least survive in another habitat.

The day that the *Academy* finally left the Galapagos for San Francisco she passed within a few miles of the point on the shore of Santa Cruz where the eight survivors of a terrible saga were facing death. They were the captain and some of the crew of the Norwegian bark *Alexandra*, who had been caught in a tragedy of the kind which had haunted the Galapagos archipelago since the time of Fray Tomás de Berlanga and Diego de Rivadeneira. Without either knowing it, the *Academy* and the marooned sailors had been shadowing each other for about five months in a deadly game of 'box and cox'.

The *Alexandra* sailed from Australia in November 1905, with a cargo of coal for Panama. The Norwegian captain, Emil Petersen, had a crew of twenty who were mostly Scandinavians too, but included two Americans, a German, a Frenchman and a Scot. They finally sighted Galera Point near Guayaquil in April 1906, after an agonisingly slow passage of five months in which the *Alexandra* had been becalmed for days and weeks on end in the Pacific doldrums. As with Bishop Berlanga all those years before, calm deadened the seas almost as soon as they came within sight of land, the sails collapsed like deflated balloons and, unknown to the weary, parched men aboard, the Humboldt current began to pull their ship inexorably away from the coast and out into the depths of the ocean. The next morning the land had disappeared once more and the *Alexandra* was drifting helplessly in the renewed and seemingly everlasting calm. The heat and dead air clamped down day after day on the ship, rocked by the swell so that her empty sails cracked and the pitch melted between the planks of the deck. The crew's rations of food and water were cut to half, and to eke out the rapidly-diminishing water supply, they tried to use the ship's condenser. After fourteen days it began to leak and then the bottom fell out of it. All that was left was a few gallons at the bottom of the tanks.

By now the crew were on the edge of mutiny. They wanted to take to the boats and row to the Galapagos Islands which were not much nearer than the mainland. The captain and first mate had to draw pistols to keep them from seizing the boats, and it was agreed that they should wait another two weeks in the hope that, even if no wind came, the current would take them to the islands. After ten days the captain spotted and identified the long shape of Albemarle Island, but once again the currents proved stronger than the occasional breath of wind, and the island disappeared.

Now the crew would not be denied. Captain Petersen warned them of the danger of leaving the ship with almost no food and water to look for islands where there might be no water either and which might be uninhabited. However, in the end he gave way to the rest of the crew. They nailed notices on the *Alexandra's* masts, explaining what they intended to do and asking anyone who found her to put in to the Galapagos to look for them. Then they abandoned ship. The captain took one long boat and the first mate the other, each with ten men. The two boats had a small iron tank apiece with about 90 litres of water, compass, sextant and some food.

Battling with powerful and unpredictable currents, the captain knew that progress would be tortuously slow. They might be swept off course faster than they could row. At the end of the second day, the men were exhausted and had lost all spirit. On the third night, the boats became separated and never saw each other again. Then the highest crater on Albemarle Island came in sight from the captain's boat, and he and his companions took some new heart, even though it was still about 40 kilometres away. One of them, Christiansen, told his story to William Beebe many years later when he had abandoned the sea to be a taxi-driver in New York:

> The cook seen it first and told us but we kept saying 'No that ain't land, it's clouds.' And he says 'No it's land,' and we'd say 'No, it's clouds,' and the captain sitting on the stern saying, 'Now boys, don't arger.' But when it got a little lighter we seen it really was land, and I want to tell you, weak as we was, them oars bent.

Finally, burnt up under the glare of the equatorial sun, they came close inshore. The breakers, and rugged lava cliffs and rocks made landing all but impossible, but they managed to find a small beach, pulled the boat on shore and leaped out eagerly.

Burnt rocks, clinkers, lava, craters, fumaroles and extinct volcanoes met their eyes, but no soil and no water. The men rushed up to the lava flows, tripping and falling on the chaotic surface. Then the sickening truth came to them: they had landed on a volcanic island which probably had no water at all. It was, in fact, the extreme southern tip of Albemarle Island.

'What now, captain?' said one of the crew. 'We must rest and then sail on to Charles' Island; according to the chart it's about fifty miles south-west of here. I know that the whalers in the old days went there for turtle and they said one could get some water there.'

So they launched their long boat again and shaped a course for Charles' Island. There was still no sign of the first mate's boat, and only a dumb obstinacy kept them going. As the next day dawned one of the crew noticed the final disaster; he shook the captain awake and showed, with a gesture of despair, that the cork in their water tank had worked loose and most of their water leaked away. They were all suffering so terribly from thirst, exhaustion and exposure, when they saw Santa Cruz ahead of them on May 20th, 1906, that they could row no more. Even if they had the strength, they could not have survived long enough to make the passage to Charles' Island. For a time it seemed that their landing place on Santa Cruz would prove to have no more water than the one on Albemarle. However, their fevered search among the tumbled lava rocks produced just enough rain water caught in small pools to satisfy their immediate thirst. It was brackish and salty with the sea spray, but drinkable enough to save dying men.

The little band may have thought that the worst of their ordeal was over. In fact it had only begun. When landing on the island desperate with thirst, they had pulled their boat some way up the sandy landing place, but not far enough. The rising tide had floated their boat on to rocks, where the surf had pounded it to pieces. There was not a piece more than a metre long to be found, and they never saw the oars again. All that remained were some pieces of clothing caught in the rocks and the empty water cask, with its top stove in. They were now trapped on the inhospitable western shore of Santa Cruz Island, with little hope left to sustain them. Although the *Alexandra*'s crew did not know it, this island was uninhabited at that time, and there was no reason for any passing ship to stop there or look for them on an island with no known source of fresh water. However, the American scientists in the *Academy* had recently found an anchorage in a protected bay on the south coast.

The wretched castaways quenched their thirst by killing seals, cutting their throats and drinking their warm blood as it gushed out. As others had done before them, they chewed the fleshy pads of cactus leaves to obtain a less-nauseating drink when they could, but not even the cactus grew everywhere. For food, they killed seals, iguanas and pelicans and later came to favour turtles. Time and again they tried to get through the lava fields which stretched everywhere, but always they were driven back. Their shoes had long ago been cut to shreds by the jagged edges of the rocks, and they used several thicknesses of seal skins lashed to their feet instead. Even these had to be replaced every few days. Christiansen described their feelings of despair:

Nights was the bad time. All day we were pretty busy . . . climbing over the rocks and watching sharp both on the land and sea sides of us. Once in a while Morrison and the Swede and I would think we sure could get inland, so we'd start off and pretty soon we'd be back, clothes torn off us, scratched and bloody, and just as wise as we was before. One day we thought we saw the smoke of a steamer but it was far off on the horizon and it never came any nearer. Nights was the worst. We'd lie there and think about things, and wonder how much longer we could drink blood instead of water; then we'd get up and look at the sea, and think where we was, and suppose a ship didn't ever come. Nights was the time we felt it.

Some of the men gave way to perpetual stupor; hopelessness and lethargy had overcome them and there was nothing left to sustain their morale. However, the tougher and more resilient spirits kept trying to find some way to salvation. Their first death struck when the only German in the crew was drowned while trying to overpower a sea turtle. Three, then four months passed. With difficulty the captain and the undefeated crew members managed to cajole the rest into making one more effort to clamber along the shoreline to find some kind of anchorage where any ship searching for them might possibly come, and a long trek began. In a small cove they found evidence of recent human occupation, a fire, a can, footprints which, though they did not know it, had been left by the *Academy*'s scientists only a few weeks before. Later in their painful stumbling progress round the southern shore of the island, another of the little band succumbed. One of the two Americans, Fred Jeff, was already weak and suffering with dysentery, and simply lay down and refused to go on. The rest of them cajoled, argued and bullied him to get up and continue with them. They stayed with him all night but Jeff was adamant and would not move: 'Rescue will come here just as soon as any other place and I will make my own way,' he said. Finally the others had to accept his decision and went on without him.

Now there were eight. Eventually they reached a high cliff encircling a bay with a smooth beach and, wonder of wonders, a little green grass and some trees. With difficulty and losing still more of their clothes in the process, they managed to cut their way inland and round to a point where it was possible to clamber down the cliff face. Beside the beach they again found evidence of recent human visitors. This was the place which had been christened 'Academy Bay' by the scientists only months before. Here the desperate survivors of the *Alexandra* found wells of brackish water, unpleasant but drinkable and plentiful. It was the nearest they had been to civilisation since November 1905. The captain said, 'Well boys, if we're ever found, we'll be found here. I don't believe there's anybody lives inland, or we'd have seen a trail or some signs in all the way we've been. This is the only harbour we've seen, there's water here, and we might just as well stay here and wait.' Academy Bay was like paradise after the rest of the island, and so the crew agreed.

After another three months, they were lying on their beach eating when one of them suddenly started to yell: 'Ship! Ship! Ship!' Then the cook took up the shout and all saw a sail coming round the east point of the bay. They jumped and started to yell and wave with joy. As they saw the ship sailing straight past they screamed, gesticulated and cried like madmen, but she kept on and went out of sight behind the island in the middle of the bay. They tried desperately to think of anything else they could do to attract attention as the sail passed from view. However, the captain of the ship knew what he was doing and, passing behind the island, kept on almost to the western point of the bay before tacking in. They had been seen and now they were saved.

The rescue ship was the *Isadora Jacinta*, sent from Guayaquil to search for them by Norwegian friends of Captain Petersen. The ship's boat containing the first mate and the other half of the *Alexandra's* crew had been picked up on the very day that the captain's group had landed on Santa Cruz. The mate had immediately given the alarm and so the search for the castaways had been in progress for months. Even so, they might never have been found. Both an Ecuadorian and a British gunboat had tried, and only found the wreck of the *Alexandra* at the south end of the island. The German captain of the *Isadora Jacinta* knew the islands better than anyone but even he had almost given up. It was only because of the treacherous Galapagos currents that he had decided to sail by Academy Bay. Those terrible currents, which had almost finished the *Alexandra's* crew, had now, ironically, saved them.

When the castaways returned to Guayaquil, some effort was made to organise an expedition to look for the wretched Fred Jeff. It was almost certainly too late already, and most of his shipmates were sure he was dead. Thirty years later, the American explorer and author Victor Wolfgang von Hagen took an expedition to the

Galapagos in January 1936, and found the skeleton of Fred Jeff 'tucked in with clinkers' on the shores of Santa Cruz.

14

The Key to Panama

A T THE TIME of their arrival in Latin America in the sixteenth century the Spaniards dreamed of cutting a canal through the isthmus of Panama to unite the Atlantic and Pacific oceans. It would have had remarkable military and commercial advantages for the royal authorities seeking to maintain some sort of order in their vast new American empire, and for the individual adventurers and soldiers of fortune who were the instruments of the conquest. The vision was magnificent but the practical capacity to tackle such an enterprise was lacking. It was to take almost four hundred years to turn the dream into reality.

As their grip on the American empire tightened, the Spanish kings from Philip II onward took a more negative attitude, and decreed that no canal or waterway should be constructed. The pressure from other European states to use it to penetrate into Spain's private world in the Pacific was too threatening, and the dream, like so many other aspirations, faded.

The colonial period of the seventeenth and eighteenth centuries did not encourage dreamers, and it was not until the arrival of Bolivar that the idea of joining the two oceans once more took hold. 'How beautiful it would be,' said Bolivar in 1826, 'if the Isthmus of Panama should become for us what the Isthmus of Corinth is to the Greeks.' To the north, as Bolivar knew, was a people who were developing the skills and the ambition to bring it about. During the rest of the nineteenth century the American interest in an all-water route across the Isthmus grew, as did that of the British and French. In 1846 the governments of the United States and of New Canada (subsequently renamed Colombia) signed a treaty which was intended to secure freedom of communications across the Isthmus of Panama and would have permitted the construction of a canal. All that ensued at that time, however, was the building of a railway across the Isthmus in 1855.

It was not until 1880 that the first attempt to build a canal actually started. Then the great French engineer, Ferdinand de Lesseps, having triumphantly completed the Suez canal, turned his attention to Panama. After ten years of struggle, the French company finally collapsed as a result of poor planning and diseases such as yellow fever, malaria and cholera, which decimated the labour force. It needed more than enterprise and engineering skill to accomplish a project of such magnitude. It would only be achieved by the intervention of a strong and determined government, and this was finally supplied by the United States administration of President Theodore Roosevelt, which came to power in 1901.

'Teddy' Roosevelt's methods have been harshly criticised both in his own time and subsequently, but they worked. The province of Panama separated from Colombia to form an independent republic in 1903, and was persuaded to sign a new treaty with the United States. This enabled the canal to be constructed through a zone of territory under American administration, with total freedom of passage for the shipping of all nations. The methods by which this was achieved may have been questionable, but the result was of untold benefit for the whole world. The construction of the canal began soon after, under Roosevelt's presidency, and it was opened for traffic in August 1914. This fateful year marked the opening of a new era for the American continent and the closing of an old one in Europe.

At the beginning of the 1890s the thoughts of some of the

maritime powers of the world, not least the United States, turned again to the Galapagos. They began to realise that, if and when the canal was built, this forgotten archipelago would for the first time in its history acquire a strategic importance for the whole continent. This created tensions, the first flicker of which was felt in 1890 when the US minister in Ecuador heard rumours that both Britain and France were again interested in acquiring a coaling station in the Galapagos. (In fact, an offer had been made in 1886 by a Mr Beck to sell Charles' Island to the British Government. What authority he had to do this is far from clear, and the authorities in London politely declined.) Subsequently, rumours began to hum that the United States was also interested in a coaling station. The United States made it clear to Europe that, while not wishing to acquire the Galapagos Islands themselves, they would not allow other powers to do so. This seems to have been a little disingenuous, because soon afterwards the United States Government was actively negotiating for them.

The islands assumed more importance as the decade advanced. In 1899 a new United States minister in Ecuador, Archibald Sampson, pointed out to Washington that the islands could have an important strategic position when the canal was built. Secretary of State Hay instructed Sampson to confine himself to discussing the possibility of acquiring facilities for a coaling station, probably on Chatham Island, and not to encourage any idea of the United States purchasing the whole of the archipelago.

Whatever the reason for Hay's caution, it was wise since the one certainty in this tangled web of national and international jealousy and ambition was that no Ecuadorian president would have got away with surrendering sovereignty over the islands. As in the 1850s, charges of giving away the nation's birthright continued to be almost standard practice for politicians in opposition. When the great liberal president, General Eloy Alfaro, came to power in 1895, his government continued this campaign of criticism against its conservative predecessors.

Nevertheless, both Ecuadorian and United States documents show that Alfaro was prepared to flirt with the idea of compromising exclusive Ecuadorian control of the Galapagos in exchange for more tangible assets. In the negotiations of 1899 the United States sought a ninety-nine-year lease of Chatham Island in exchange for a rent of five thousand dollars per year. Alfaro was prepared to grant such a lease, but in return wanted a United States guarantee of Ecuador's sovereignty over the islands as a whole, and a great deal more money. He told Archibald Sampson, by way of opening the bidding, that a European syndicate had offered twenty-five million dollars for the whole of the archipelago; and that France would give one hundred million francs in return for the opening of a free port (a remarkably generous offer if, as Alfaro claimed, it was to be available to the trade of the whole world). At a later stage, the French offer was said to have risen to three hundred million francs for the entire group, and President Alfaro told the Americans that in his opinion the major islands were worth about fifty million dollars each. The difference between the opening United States offer and Ecuador's asking price was too great to be bridged. There was some talk of a bargain in which the United States would provide a warship and other military supplies in part payment, but ultimately France sold Ecuador a gunboat and the negotiations with the United States collapsed.

Minister Sampson persisted, and in 1903 he suggested that Chatham Island might be purchased outright for one to two million dollars. When this was considered in Washington it appeared that the US Navy was no longer interested, despite the fact that the very same year the Panama Canal had begun to look like a practical proposition, following the conclusion of the new treaty between the United States and the Republic of Panama. A new president, Leonidas Plaza Gutiérrez, had succeeded Eloy Alfaro in Ecuador and, faced with the usual financial crisis, he put out feelers to Washington about the possibility of a loan of ten million dollars to be secured by a 'mortgage' on the islands. Sampson stipulated that the United States should actually have possession of the islands during the term of the loan, and once more negotiations petered out inconclusively. However, Plaza had appreciated that Theodore Roosevelt's blunt use of American power to secure undisputed possession of the Panama canal zone was capable of being repeated. He warned his countrymen of the threat posed by 'the wave from the North', arguing that the only practical defence against this pressure was to concede something and 'make room' for United States commercial interests.

Eloy Alfaro returned to power in 1906, and soon initiated new negotiations with another US Minister, Mr Lee, through an intermediary, Miguel Alburquerque, without securing a definite offer from Washington. The State Department official who dealt with the matter annotated Lee's request for instructions with a succinct statement of the normal, although not invariable, US policy: 'We don't want them ourselves and won't allow any European (or extra-American) power to acquire control of them.'

The issue arose again in 1908 when Chile expressed interest in acquiring territory, or at least coaling facilities, in the archipelago. When this was discussed in Washington the Secretary of State, Elihu Root, pointed out that the Galapagos had a strategic position 'whence all the North-West Coast of South America could be dominated' and said that while there would be no objection to a Chilean purchase, the United States could not permit the islands to be occupied by any other than an American country. Root apparently preferred the status quo, and the Chilean proposal was not carried forward.

Three years later President Alfaro received a proposal from the United States involving a ninety-nine-year lease of the islands for a price of fifteen million dollars and a United States' guarantee of Ecuador's territorial integrity. This was a huge price, almost twice the sum which the United States had paid for the whole of Alaska. Alfaro weighed the dangers of toying with such proposals against the fact that the possession of the Galapagos involved Ecuador, however reluctantly, in the strategic power game centred henceforth on the Panama canal. He reported the new proposal in a message of January 16th, 1911, which carefully explained the dilemma to all the provincial governors in the country.

Although the islands had until then been a liability to Ecuador, their position in relation to Panama would make them a great potential asset once the canal was opened. Her sovereignty over the archipelago would very soon, therefore, involve Ecuador in a most delicate international problem. 'The solution of problems of that kind,' Alfaro wryly added, 'is very seldom advantageous for the weaker nations.' He went on to ask the governors to consult opinion in their provinces about the proposal, on the basis of his cabinet's plan for spending the fifteen million dollars. This was a nicely-balanced scheme for distributing a reasonable slice of the cake to each part of the country: much needed sanitation in Guayaquil, and roads or railways for the northern, southern and even the Amazonic regions. However, these attractive offers could not quieten the patriotic and nationalistic opposition and, like so many earlier proposals, the offer of 1911 foundered on those rocks.

Eloy Alfaro's message, a mixture of wishful thinking and realism, is one of the few full accounts of an Ecuadorian president's view on the Galapagos. He says that the resources of cod in the area were much richer than those in Newfoundland (for which he had no evidence at all) and that the islands would one day be the port of call for all shipping passing through Panama (which they have never been and hardly could be). On the other hand, he recognises that Ecuador could not defend them and, if war broke out, might see them occupied by a superior force. 'For us,' he concluded, 'the archipelago is a distant hope but an immediate danger.'

The Galapagos have remained under sole Ecuadorian sovereignty ever since and it was to the long-term advantage of the United States that she never acquired any permanent base there, let alone sovereignty. The view expressed by Secretary Elihu Root in 1908 seems fundamentally right. After World War I, the British

Government published in a strategic assessment (*Peace Handbook*, 1919) that:

> the very considerable cost of defending a base in the Galapagos group would not in truth have been worth while. In time of war, the Galapagos group, like any other widespread collection of islands, would be liable to attack by an enemy cruiser at many points, and correspondingly difficult to defend. They would not be worth fortifying and providing with a garrison; and, without these precautions, a coal depot at any one of them would but tempt an enemy raider... Commodious harbours in the full sense are almost non-existent; roadsteads with good anchorages and shelter are few; and fresh water is scarce.

The islands seem to have been forgotten by the combatants in the 1914–18 war. It was suggested by Don Carlos Manuel Larrea, author of the definitive history of the Galapagos, that one of the famous Imperial German naval commanders of that war, Graf von Luckner, used them as a hide-out for his raids on British and Allied shipping in a similar way to Captain David Porter, but von Luckner did not confirm this. Ecuador was able without difficulty to maintain her (admittedly nominal) control and the neutral status of her possession. Alfredo Baquerizo Moreno celebrated the fact by paying the first presidential visit to the islands in 1916. The event is remembered now by the new name, Puerto Baquerizo Moreno, given to the chief port and capital of Chatham Island. The political custom in Ecuador and most other sensibly governed countries is that a presidential visit is the occasion for tangible favours, not only formal honours, to be bestowed on the place visited. President Baquerizo probably followed this popular custom; but since there were still not more than three hundred inhabitants, the cost could not have been too high.

The lack of enthusiasm shown by both the United States and British navies for establishing a coaling station or other facilities for warships is explained in the above extract from the British assessment published in 1919. However, the strategic relationship of the Galapagos to the Panama canal was equally obvious, and the rise of Japanese power and ambition in the Pacific between the two wars was a continual source of concern to the United States.

The Galapagos were commonly described as 'the Achilles heel of the Panama Canal', and it was known that Japanese fishing boats constantly visited the area. There was an obvious risk of their occupying undefended islands lying less than 1,500 kilometres from Panama. During this period there were frequent American naval visits, and the islands often featured (without permission, to the irritation of the Ecuadorian government) in US naval exercises. Washington's close interest and concern was most vividly shown in 1938, when President Franklin Roosevelt personally visited the islands on board the USS *Houston*. However, not even this visit produced any decisive action to secure the Galapagos against occupation by an unfriendly power.

One of the American writers who agitated for action from Washington in the uneasy period of gathering storm in the 1930s was Victor Wolfgang von Hagen. He led an expedition to the Galapagos in 1935 to mark the centenary of Charles Darwin's visit, and erected a statue to him on Chatham Island. Having paid homage to Darwin, von Hagen and his companions stayed on to add their contribution to the biological study which was, and still is, unfinished. Von Hagen was one of the first to press hard for effective measures of conservation for Galapagos wildlife. A year previously, the Ecuador national assembly had passed the first legislation to protect certain species on certain islands, but it was largely a vain gesture because there was no means of enforcing the law on the islands. Von Hagen's fertile mind conceived the idea of a scientific research station on the spot to serve as the centre and instrument of conservation. He ingeniously suggested that the US Navy should give financial and practical help in establishing the research station, provide it with a vessel, radio and so on, in return for which the scientists would provide maritime as well as zoological surveillance reports: in other words, two birds (and any number of gunboats and other species) could be killed with one stone. Unfortunately, the navy did not take to the idea, and it was another twenty-five years before the research station was founded.

At the outbreak of World War II Ecuadorian public opinion was as fiercely opposed as ever to giving up sovereignty over the Galapagos. However, two new factors were about to transform the situation. First, the advent of air warfare made it even more vital to deny the islands to an enemy who might use them as an advance air base within a few hours of the canal. Second, the Japanese attack on Pearl Harbour in December 1941 and their successes in South East Asia, made it apparent to every country in the Americas that all were now under real threat. The shock of war concentrated minds in both the United States and the Latin American republics. It was clear to them all that the Panama Canal, a life line for the Pacific seaboard states of both continents, might at any moment be attacked by Japan, and the Galapagos Islands could be used as both a shield and a base for such an attack. In this state of emergency, the government of Ecuador promptly agreed to grant the United States the use of South Seymour Island.

Starting in the summer of 1942, the United States Sixth Air Force constructed a complete air base on South Seymour. Engineers blasted the lava clear to create an airfield, including two 1,800 metre landing strips. Quonset hut cantonments, maintenance bays, water distillation plant and all the paraphernalia of modern warfare sprang up on the low-lying waste land and, for the first time since Captain Porter's visit in 1812, the Stars and Stripes flew over the island. South Seymour was turned into an unsinkable aircraft carrier from which the distant approaches to Panama were guarded, and a watch maintained for submarine and other threats to shipping in a key sector of the Pacific. Von Hagen called it a beach-head on the moon, and the men stationed there called it the Rock and so named their newspaper, the first ever published in the

Galapagos. They found service in the red dust of the Galapagos a monotonous grind, but it was preferable to the fate of the troops who were faced with the task of pushing the Japanese back from island to island across the Pacific. The goats, sea-lions, and land and sea iguanas, with whom the airmen shared the barren lava, were unable to fight back.

However, the air base on South Seymour (Baltra) has had a considerable impact on the social and economic life of the islands even after the closure of the base in 1947. Each householder in the islands was allowed to remove one of the clapboard wooden buildings from the base for his own use, so that until recently the majority of the buildings in the main villages on the islands were made from materials taken from the base. The main runway of the base was resurfaced and the Ecuadorian Airforce established its own base there. There are now five flights a week and the airstrip is the island's main link to the mainland, and the entry point for the majority of visitors.

15

Murder in Paradise

WILLIAM BEEBE CAME TWICE to the Galapagos islands in the 1920s, and recorded his first visit in a superb book called *Galapagos: World's End*, which became a bestseller in the United States and several other countries. Beebe arrived with a highly organised (but still very human) team of scientists from the New York Zoological Society in the *Noma*, which had been expensively converted from a luxury yacht into a base and floating laboratory for an intensive and determined scientific assault on the Galapagos. The *Noma* was unfortunately a steam yacht and needed large quantities of coal and fresh water to keep going. Neither commodity being easy to come by on the islands, the ship had to spend a great deal of time steaming from place to place to find them, and the frustrated scientists spent more time gazing at their objectives from the rail than actually ashore studying them at close quarters. This elaborately prepared expedition involved a grand total, as Beebe himself put it, of about 6,000 minutes (not much more than four days) ashore.

Beebe was the first to see the funny side of the affair. The *Noma* was provided with every imaginable luxury and the finest research facilities which money could buy. Dampier and Darwin had nothing like these advantages, being lucky if they had a flat surface to work on and could manage to keep their paper dry. The *Noma* had steam engines and could sail serenely above all the maddening delays caused by winds and currents in the past. But, for all her technological superiority, the *Noma* was hardly more effective in the Galapagos. The search for water became the principal concern of the expedition. Salt water damaged the ship's modern boilers, and fresh water was, of course, scarce. At one stage, they began to steam about the islands in pursuit of any rain clouds they could see forming in the distance, hoping to overtake them and catch the rain. Searching for water, they burned up so much coal that they had to return to Panama for more. However, Beebe and his team made up with energy and enthusiasm for their lack of research time when they finally got ashore. They threw themselves with total commitment into their work and emerged at the end of their stay with respectable, if not outstanding, achievements to their credit. Beebe listed these as ninety watercolours, four hundred photographs, one hundred and sixty bird skins, one hundred and fifty reptiles, two hundred fish, two thousand insects, forty jars of specimens, sixty jars of plankton, two hundred microscopic slides and one hundred specimens of plants: no mean feat for four days' work. However, the real and abiding achievement which Beebe and his friends have given us is the vivid impressions of the islands set down in the book.

William Beebe's book struck chords all round the world and many of his readers wanted to go to the Galapagos, however difficult it might be. The appeal was strongest in Norway, at the opposite end of the world from Ecuador, where the book was an instant success. Large numbers of Norwegians were captured by the romance of the islands and an Oslo promoter, improbably called Harry Randall, saw an opportunity to exploit their imaginations. Randall set up a colonising enterprise in 1927, presenting the islands as an earthly paradise with the finest climate in the world, plentiful water and enough fertile soil to produce food for one hundred thousand people.

Each member of the scheme had to put up four thousand

kroners and two thousand more for their wives. This was Randall's profit. The poor victims also invested in cows, chickens, seeds, tools, timber, a tractor, fishing equipment and, since Randall hinted that 'diamonds may be found', drilling gear. With high hopes they landed on Charles' Island, where Patrick Watkins, Villamil and Valdizán had failed before. The ruins of their efforts could still be seen and were a poor augury for the Norwegian colony. One glance at the cactus-studded land told them that they had been duped and brought, all too literally, to the end of the world by false promises.

Norwegians are not easily beaten, and they set to and built frame houses and roads, tried to create reservoirs by damming the water sources, set up a fish cannery and planted crops. However, the odds were too great and the community started to break up; many died, some returned home or to the mainland, and some took to drink. Another group arrived and set up on Chatham. This colony fared no better, and after two years there was only one family left on Charles' and three men on Chatham. A final attempt at Academy Bay on Santa Cruz ended, like so many others, in death. The boiler of the new Norwegian fish cannery blew up, killing two of the men. By 1929 there were only three left there, and the scandal, denunciations, and law suits had reached such a pitch that the cabinet in Oslo fell and the Ecuadorian authorities seized the greater part of the remaining assets.

By 1929 the last of the Norwegians had gone, leaving behind them only flourishing populations of wild cattle, pigs, and dogs, and groves of oranges, papayas, and lemons from which new settlers could benefit. Undeterred by the grim history of earlier settlements, a few hopeful Europeans now started to arrive again. They were to become the dramatis personae in a murder story worthy of Agatha Christie, and in fact, remarkably similar to her classic detective novel *Ten Little Niggers*. But this story is true.

In August 1929 an odd German couple landed at Post Office Bay in the north of Charles' Island. They were Dr Friedrich Ritter and his companion, Dore Strauch, both married to other partners who had stayed behind in Germany. While Dore was unashamedly in love with her new man, Friedrich professed to have little or no interest in transient human affections. His purpose was to create a new and totally independent life in which, freed from all mundane pressures, he could devote himself to contemplation and to his life's task of writing on philosophy. It was, indeed, a common admiration for the philosophy of Nietzsche that had brought the two together in the first place. In her book about their life together in the Galapagos, *Satan came to Eden*, Dore Strauch says she would not 'go into the details of Dr Ritter's philosophy . . . but it is necessary perhaps, in order to give a clear picture of him at that time, to say that it moved between two poles, with Nietzsche at the one end, and at the other Laotse.' It was not a good basis for meeting the demands of life on a desert island. Neither Dore nor anyone else ever succeeded in grasping the meaning of the philosophical synthesis which Ritter was striving to produce. Fortunately for both of them, he proved to be a lot more practical in coping with the day-to-day demands of life on Charles' Island than might be expected of a vegetarian, nudist pseudo-philosopher.

By 1932, Ritter and Strauch had established themselves in a permanent home called Friedo, an elision of their own names, which they had built by a good spring on the western side of the island. They were able to support themselves tolerably with the fruit and vegetables they grew in their large plot of land, supplemented by eggs; and occasionally when vegetarian principles had to give way to necessity, the meat of the wild cattle which their predecessors had left to roam freely. On several occasions they were visited by curious parties from American yachts who gave them invaluable tools and supplies, and this help was gratefully accepted. The Ritters claimed to be glad that various groups of Germans who tried to establish themselves on Charles' as permanent residents failed and left. In August 1932 however, a new group of Germans arrived to stay.

Heinz and Margret Wittmer and Harry, his twelve-year-old son and her stepson, had left Cologne because they had been advised that Harry's delicate health and very bad eyesight could be cured only by spending two years in a sanatorium. Feeling that they could not possibly afford this, Heinz and Margret decided to spend a few years in the peaceful and, as they thought, healthy environment of the Galapagos, which they hoped would prove an equally good therapy for Harry. It was an odder motive even than Ritter's for coming to the Galapagos. There were many other isolated places where the Wittmers could more easily have led a simple and largely self-sufficient life with an invalid son. In fact, few could have been so remote and unsuitable for their purpose as the Galapagos. The cost of getting three people out there with the large quantities of equipment and supplies they brought, could not have been much less than the cost of sending Harry to a sanatorium in Germany, where, in addition, Heinz Wittmer would have been able to continue earning a living. According to Margret, he had a good job as secretary to Dr Konrad Adenauer, then *Oberburgermeister* of Cologne.

In their very different ways Ritter and Strauch and the Wittmers had set out to make new, free and private lives for themselves away from the menace and tension of Europe in the 1930s. Neither group had planned to share this life with other people, and Ritter, apparently was so engrossed in his philosophical studies and the physical struggle to establish his little kingdom, that he had very little time to spare even for his chosen woman companion. Yet, with an ominous inevitability, the two couples seemed to gravitate towards each other. The Wittmers made the first move. As the new arrivals, they were more in need of practical help and advice, and Margret Wittmer was pregnant. Believing that Ritter was a qualified doctor, they asked him straightaway if he would help to deliver the baby when the time came. According to Dore, Friedrich Ritter had been a successful physician in Berlin. The other contemporary inhabitants of Charles' Island described him, less flatteringly, as a dentist or a dental technician, but he was undoubtedly the only person there with any medical knowledge at all, and the Wittmers were counting on his help. Ritter, perhaps the most determined as well as the most eccentric of all the settlers, flatly refused to promise any help at all.

This bad start was made worse by the fact that the two women hated each other with cordial wholeheartedness from the moment they met. Both Dore and Margret wrote lengthy books about their Galapagos adventures, and both are full of damning criticisms of the other. Dore's version of the first meeting was that Heinz Wittmer called by himself on the well-advertised nudists, dressed only in a pair of shorts. 'Friedrich and I behaved as hospitably as we could towards this curiously-attired person, but it could not be helped if we showed him somewhat clearly that his get-up had not won our sympathy!' Margret Wittmer, on the other hand, insists that she and her husband called together, she in her best dress, and that Dore made fun of her for being overdressed in the Galapagos. Dore tried to go 'one up' by plunging into talk about Nietzsche, which might have disconcerted almost anyone. Margret was a plain German *hausfrau* and, although she later acquired a taste for fame and name-dropping, she was completely baffled by philosophy. Her interests in 1932 were confined to the practical problems of homemaking on desert islands.

After this the two couples kept their distance from each other most of the time. The men had plenty on their hands, sweating to raise their vegetables and protect them from the wild pigs and cattle, to build their houses and to get some kind of tolerable living for themselves in their stony paradise, and so they hardly had time to quarrel. Dore thought that no one less self-reliant and imbued with Nietzschean willpower than herself and Friedrich could possibly stand the island for very long.

The oddest thing about these two ill-assorted couples was that, despite their professed determination to live pure and simple lives on their desert island (and Ritter's fury at having to share it with anyone at all), they were hypnotised by the lure of publicity.

Margret Wittmer, the least likely to look beyond her family circle, had brought a typewriter rather than a sewing machine to the Galapagos. Before the Wittmers arrived, Friedrich Ritter had written a series of articles in 1931 about his and Dore's life in the Galapagos for the American magazine, *Atlantic Monthly*. They were rather dull articles, with appetising titles, such as 'Adam and Eve in Galapagos', 'Satan walks in the Garden' and 'Eve calls it a Day'. These titles were strangely prophetic, because a self-appointed Eve was about to arrive in the Garden of Eden in the person of the Baroness Eloise Wagner-Bousquet. The Baroness and her friends were perhaps the most bizarre, and certainly the most notorious, of all the migratory human beings who have ever reached the islands. She claimed to be an Austrian aristocrat with a glittering past in Vienna who had married a distinguished Frenchman. She had, however, mislaid Monsieur Bousquet somewhere on her way to the islands, and came instead with two consorts called Philippson and Lorenz and an Ecuadorian factotum named Valdivieso. Other men appeared on the scene from time to time.

If there had been friction between the two families already living on the 250 square kilometres of Charles' Island, it was as nothing compared with the battles which now began. The Baroness had planned to build a luxury hotel to be named Paradise Regained – for the benefit of the American millionaires who were beginning to arrive in some strength each year in the wake of William Beebe. The building was never started, but the Baroness made it very clear that she regarded herself as queen of the island and eventually declared herself no less than 'Empress of Floreana'. While she could not entirely override the prior claims established by the Wittmers, and Ritter and Strauch, she and her henchmen drove off all other intruders, on occasions at gunpoint. By right of her aristocratic origins and superior fire power, she appropriated any available property for herself, and set out to dominate the life of Charles' Island.

Publicity became a major source of trouble among the 'ten little niggers'. Until the arrival of the Baroness, Ritter had enjoyed a monopoly. The press were interested in his lovelife and his nudist and vegetarian views, rather than in his philosophical studies. What caught the popular imagination particularly was that he had had all his teeth extracted before leaving Germany and had made himself a strong set of steel dentures: an unusual, but perhaps practical, precaution on a desert island. However much he might protest against the invasion of his privacy, the fact remains that he sought and won for himself a niche in the international press.

When the Baroness arrived she swept him from the limelight. She was a gift to the popular press, both by her way of life and by her deliberate efforts to supply what the public liked to read on a Sunday morning. As the Galapagos were so far away and definite information was lacking, there was nothing to restrain the wildest flights of journalistic imagination. Her harem of young males, the horsewhip she carried in her hand and the pistol in her belt provided splendid copy. Her autocratic actions such as driving off a honeymoon couple who arrived one day in a small boat, inevitably led to screaming headlines such as 'Revolution on Pacific Island', 'Baroness seizes control of Galapagos island' and 'Woman proclaims herself Empress'.

Meanwhile, Frau Wittmer was not only last in the social pecking order, but, having no visible eccentricities to sell, was overlooked by the press and found no profitable employment for her typewriter. Both Margret and Dore came to hate the Baroness more fiercely than they disliked one another.

The male harem did not stay together for very long: one left quite early after a quarrel; another when he was shot in the stomach. Dr Ritter reported to the local authorities that the medical evidence proved that the Baroness fired the shot. She denied that the shot was even from her gun, and nothing was ever done about the matter. The harem was now reduced to the two Germans, Philippson and Lorenz. Their status was obscure for the Baroness often referred to Philippson as her 'husband', though

Lorenz seemed to have been the reigning gigolo when they first arrived. The three of them shared a cabin which they erected near the Wittmers' spring, and called it Hacienda Paradise. There was just as much trouble within this paradise as between the Baroness's group and the others. Before long Lorenz was not only superseded by Philippson as favourite, but began to be treated as the scullion, made to do all the menial tasks and beaten when he failed to please. He did not get a fair share of the food, and, whether from physical or emotional causes, grew sick and emaciated.

In January 1933 the Wittmers' baby, Rolf, was born, bringing the number of colonists to nine, and late in that year the tragedies began. One night, Lorenz took refuge with the Wittmers. Margret was reluctant to take him in because she had come to the conclusion that the Baroness and Philippson were insane, and she was afraid of what they might do to anyone protecting their victim. 'His groans and their shrill abuse sometimes penetrated to us from Paradise.' However, when he finally arrived, weeping like a child, she says she found it impossible to refuse him. This happened during what was a trying period for everyone on Charles'. Even in the normally cool and humid uplands where the three groups lived, no rain fell for months on end. The heat was unbearable, the animals died, the crops withered and the vital springs dwindled almost to nothing. As the searing and demoralising drought dragged on into 1934, the strains generated by hatred and jealousy became unbearable and something cracked.

Margret Wittmer was alone in the house when the Baroness called one day in March and asked to see Lorenz. He was out and she said she could not wait for him to return, because friends had come in their yacht and were taking Phillippson and herself to Tahiti, where they would have better prospects for starting their hotel. Would Frau Wittmer tell Lorenz to look after anything she left behind until she returned or sent instructions?

When she gave Lorenz this message, his reaction was: 'It's a trap to lure me down there, and when I get there, they'll bump me off. I know too much about her.' This seemed an odd reaction as, according to Margret, Lorenz had been going 'down there' regularly the whole time he lived with the Wittmer family, and on this occasion the Baroness had not actually suggested that he should go. Despite his intense fears and the fact that he had not been invited, Margret Wittmer claimed that he eventually summoned up his courage and set off for Paradise. She did not see Lorenz again for two days. When he returned he told her that he had found the hut deserted and most of the contents gone. He could find no trace of a ship or of the Baroness and Philippson except 'some footprints in the sand'. Why he should have spent two days hunting for them, if he believed they had left by sea, is not explained.

When Ritter and Strauch heard the news, Dore danced for joy, but Ritter was incredulous. He had seen no ship, though admittedly he could only see one of the two anchorages from his home. (The Wittmers could see neither from their place.) Margret Wittmer states that Ritter insisted most officiously on drawing up a report for the authorities, embodying all the evidence available.

> We had no objection to her departure being recorded, though it dawned on us later that he was decidedly anxious to set himself up as the island's legal authority, guardian of law and order... It struck us again what a hurry he seemed to be in to put in writing what was after all far from proven fact.

Frau Wittmer was the sole source of the story that the Baroness had said she was leaving for Tahiti, for no one else had been present when the Baroness came to leave her message for Lorenz. Nobody saw the ship at Charles' Island and no visiting yacht was reported anywhere in the Galapagos. The Baroness never reached Tahiti. No ship ever reported carrying her as a passenger, though her disappearance aroused worldwide interest. The 'friends' who came to take her away remained silent, and nothing more has ever been heard of the Baroness and Philippson. The only reasonable conclusion is that they never left the island.

Did the Baroness invent the story of the voyage to Tahiti? There is no reason for thinking she was a devotee of truth but, as she was living close to the Wittmers, it seems pointless that she should lie about leaving in a non-existent yacht, when she would still be on the island for all to see. There is also the extraordinary coincidence that, although it appears there was no yacht, the Baroness and Philippson did disappear that very day as completely as if they had sailed off into the Pacific.

Margret Wittmer implies that Friedrich Ritter knew something about the mystery. She says that all the others hurried over to Paradise where 'Ritter opened up the crates and boxes with complete assurance', as though he definitely knew that the Baroness would never return. She adds that he bought whatever of the Baroness's and Philippson's belongings he fancied from Lorenz, while Heinz bought what was left. In fact, the Wittmers seem to have got most of it, including the materials with which the cabin itself was built. Nobody worried much about the possibility of the redoubtable Baroness coming back, otherwise the Wittmers would hardly have dared to dismantle her home. Frau Wittmer says that 'sinister suspicions long pushed to the back of our minds began to come to the surface,' and that she and Heinz began to discuss possible ways in which Lorenz might have killed his tormentors and disposed of their bodies. Dore Strauch believed that the Wittmers had helped him. Lorenz himself left no first-hand account of what happened.

In April, when the drought finally broke on Charles', the series of tragedies had only just begun. Whatever part he had played, Lorenz was now anxious to leave the island. When a Swedish explorer, Rolf Blomberg, arrived a few months later in the rather decrepit fishing boat *Dinamita*, owned by the Norwegian, Trygve

Nuggeröd, he begged them to take him with them to Santa Cruz. There he hoped to find another ship and, failing to do so, he persuaded Nuggeröd to take him on to Chatham Island.

This was the *Dinamita's* last voyage. Whether the motor broke down or the fuel ran out will never be known, but it is clear that the little boat was carried helplessly in the current to Bindloe, one of the more northerly islands of the archipelago. Many weeks later American fishing boats saw a white rag fluttering by the shore. They found the *Dinamita's* dinghy and the mummified bodies of Lorenz and Nuggeröd on the beach, where they had died of thirst. The boat and a young Ecuadorian deckhand had disappeared without trace.

With the Baroness and all her original party out of the reckoning, only six 'little niggers' were left. In November, four months after Lorenz's death, Dore Strauch struggled over to the Wittmers to ask their help, for she thought Ritter was dying. Both women described the deathbed scene in detail, but their accounts differ markedly.

For Dore Strauch life on Charles' Island had not worked out as delightfully as she had expected. Her relationship with Ritter in these harsh conditions proved unexpectedly difficult as 'every trace of tenderness departed from Friedrich's attitude once they had settled on the island.' She loved flowers but Friedrich objected to them as 'foolish decoration'. She disobeyed him and planted seeds. When she fell ill and begged him to water her plants, he went out and tore them all up. For philosophical reasons he would not let her have a child, and as a disciple of Nietzsche and the power of the will, he tried only to dominate.

In spite of the bitterness of her solitude, Dore seems to have been incapable of finding an escape in the company of other women. She was attracted to the Baroness – 'at least she was no little bourgeois *Hausfrau*' – but the Baroness wanted to lord it over her, and so she hated her too. For five years she was without any emotional outlet, but by the autumn of 1934 Dore claimed that 'Friedrich had become considerate and tender. All storms had ceased. A stillness and happiness that we had never known before united us in that last month in more than human oneness.'

According to Frau Wittmer, Ritter died of meat poisoning, and she put real gusto into deriding the hypocrisy of this backsliding vegetarian. She says that Heinz saw Friedrich potting chickens which had died of poisoning; he insisted that, with a good boiling, the meat would be perfectly edible. When Margret reached his bedside, his tongue was so swollen that he could not speak and had to write what he wanted to say. She says it was too late to save him because Dore had delayed calling her. Dore, on the other hand, says that Ritter died after a stroke. He asked her to give him his revolver, but she refused as she thought he would recover. It does seem almost incredible that a man with medical knowledge should insist on eating obviously tainted meat, but Dr Ritter was a very odd, as well as a very opinionated, man. No doubt Dore would have been unwilling to admit that the much-publicised vegetarian had died of meat poisoning, and she claimed that she, too, had eaten some of the meat and was none the worse for it.

Margret Wittmer speculates at some length on the possibilities that Dore poisoned Friedrich, or that she deliberately refused to seek help until she knew it was too late, admitting that 'all this was mere conjecture, of course'. She insists that Friedrich's 'last emotion' was hatred for Dore and that he raised himself on his bed with a last desperate effort, glared at Dore 'his eyes gleaming with hate' and wrote on a piece of paper: 'I curse you with my dying breath.' Dore Strauch could not challenge this account, as she died long before Margret Wittmer wrote it. Her own version of Friedrich's end was: 'Suddenly he opened his great blue eyes and stretched his arms towards me; his glance was joyously tranquil.' To us now, both versions may ring false, for we are not filled by the same intense emotions which these two women felt as they relived their experiences in that fateful year.

Soon afterwards, the American tycoon, Allan Hancock, arrived once more in his yacht, *Velero III*. He had received a letter from

Ritter asking him to come quickly because dreadful things had happened that he could not put into a letter, as he had no proof. Hancock arrived too late to hear the full story of Ritter's suspicions, and all he could do was to take Dore Strauch away from the island. She returned to Germany where she had Ritter's writings published as well as her own book, *Satan came to Eden*.

Thus when the governor of the Galapagos arrived to make his official enquiry nearly ten months after the disappearance of the Baroness, the only people left on the island were the Wittmers. Now there were four. The governor bluntly accused Heinz Wittmer of having killed the Baroness and Philippson. He apparently based his charge on a communication that Ritter had made before his death. Margret says that they had little difficulty in refuting this, and the governor accepted their statements, and, indeed, there was no formal trial. She suggests, without undue delicacy, that Ritter had a hand in the murders: 'He may well have at least encouraged Lorenz to carry out the crime; perhaps more.' When she published *Floreana* a quarter of a century after the events, her deep loathing for the Ritters was still manifest every time she mentioned them. She made fun of Friedrich's teeth, derided him as a lapsed vegetarian and nudist, scorned his 'pretentious outpourings of pseudo-scientific philosophy' and, above all, showed her abiding hatred for the man who 'tried with such meanness and malice to drive us out of our beautiful island', so that he could be the only recipient of American gifts. Apart from this, the book contains no evidence that would incriminate Ritter in the disappearance of the Baroness and her companion.

Everyone on the island had cause enough to hate the Baroness, and thought it would be a better place without her. Possibly Lorenz had the strongest motive after the way he had been treated. However, the others had deep grudges against her, particularly the Wittmers, as she had installed herself so close to their little spring. There were three men, two women, and a fourteen-year-old boy, who might theoretically have done the deed, though the boy was half-blind. Ritter was the least likely suspect, not so much because he lived further away or liked the Baroness any better, but because of his behaviour throughout the events. From the beginning he refused to believe the story that the Baroness had gone to Tahiti, yet if he had been involved in her death, the story would have provided him with admirable cover. It was Ritter who provoked the enquiry into her death, though he was dead by the time it took place.

This leaves Lorenz, Dore and the Wittmers. Heinz Wittmer was hardy, and habitually hunted wild cattle and boars with his rifle. Lorenz was weak, sick and, it seems, cowardly. It has been argued that he was incapable of killing Philippson and the Baroness, and altogether too feeble to dispose of their bodies, but this is far from certain. There is such a thing as the courage of despair, and in the Galapagos there are ways of dealing with corpses that are not available in most places. Suppose, for instance, that his two tormentors were bathing, leaving their revolvers on the beach. It would not require expert marksmanship to kill them in the water, and the sharks would do the rest. Alternatively, if they had wandered off the beaten track, the broken lava is full of places where bodies would never be found. So, any of the suspects could have killed the Baroness and Philippson, with or without help.

In his recent account of this story, *The Galapagos Affair*, which is certainly the most thorough so far, John Treherne has given us what he regards as the most likely hypothesis. There could be others but this holds the field until new evidence turns up, which could still happen.

As we have seen, it is difficult to trace with certainty the truth of the events that led to the disappearance of the Baroness and Philippson and the poisoning of Ritter. However, the following hypothesis is feasible. The Baroness, together with Philippson, really did call on Margret Wittmer, and told her that they were about to depart on a yacht for a cruise. This story was a subterfuge to lure Lorenz back to the Hacienda Paradiso. Lorenz was not fooled, but, instead, managed to kill the Baroness and Philippson, by unknown means, most probably on March 27th or 28th, 1934. Friedrich Ritter would have been his most likely accomplice. Dore Strauch's relationship with Friedrich had deteriorated to such an extent that she sought Lorenz's company and, therefore, knew of his dispatch of the Baroness and Philippson, or alternatively, learned from Friedrich of his own involvement. Dore poisoned Ritter most probably as a result of a culinary accident or an unpremeditated act of malice or, very much less likely, as a calculated act.

It is a denouement worthy of Agatha Christie at the top of her form.

Long after, there was another strange case of a disappearing woman not far from the Wittmer's home. In 1963 Mrs Reiser, an elderly American lady, landed on Charles' Island from a cruise ship. She was walking up the trail with friends when she stopped to remove a stone from her shoe, telling the others she would catch up with them. She was never seen again. Communications with the Galapagos had improved immeasurably since the Baroness's disappearance, and the US Embassy was alerted, search parties were organised and a helicopter was sent to join in the hunt, but it was all in vain. In 1981 her remains were discovered. It seemed likely that she had simply lost her way and died of exhaustion and dehydration.

Frau Wittmer was to be involved in yet another mystery. By now she had two children, both grown up. Her daughter had married an Ecuadorian, who came to live with them on Charles' Island, and he too disappeared. Frau Wittmer said that he went off with his donkey to collect firewood, and the donkey came back but he did not. This time the authorities acted. She was arrested and taken to Chatham for interrogation, together with her son and her hired labourer. After ten days they were all released and returned to Charles' Island. No further explanation has been forthcoming and the son-in-law's body has never been found.

The combined deaths of the Baroness, Philippson, Lorenz and Ritter in such strange circumstances led to tremendous press interest, and Frau Wittmer returned to Germany to write for the newspapers, and give lectures about her strange experiences, but after a year's absence she returned to Charles' Island which she preferred to life in Germany. The years after the nightmare of 1934 were the best from her point of view: 'I like very much to live on Floreana alone,' she bluntly told Frances Conway, a later and more temporary settler.

So, the only one of the original 'ten little niggers' left is still there. Rolf, who was born on the island just a few weeks before the disappearance of the Baroness, still lives in the Galapagos and is captain of one of the yachts which visitors can charter to visit the islands. Sometimes he will take his passengers to Charles' to visit his mother, and enjoy her solid German cooking. For approaching two decades, Margret has reigned over her little kingdom, meeting the rich and the famous when they have passed her way and enjoying every minute of it, a big fish in a small pond. Her greatest achievement is to have survived the strains of life in the tough environment of a desert island. Conditions which defeated intellectual misfits like Ritter and social oddities like the Baroness could not overcome the solid virtues of a German *hausfrau* with the will to outlast all others.

16

Conservation of Species

W E HAVE SEEN HOW THE depredation of the whalers and the first settlers were threatening the Galapagos at the time of Darwin's visit in 1835, and the situation worsened over the next 100 years. As the nineteenth century progressed other scientific expeditions were organised, although the long and difficult journey round Cape Horn restricted both their number and duration. With the opening of the Panama Canal, access became easier and the Galapagos attracted a series of rich North American amateurs who invited scientists to go with them as guests. Slowly the reports and scientific findings of these visits, and particularly William Beebe's best-selling book, *Galapagos, World's End*, made the Galapagos fauna and flora known to the world. People were aware of the threat to the ecology of the islands but the concept of environmental conservation was still restricted to a few zealots, and no existing organisations covered such remote areas as the Galapagos. Meanwhile continued efforts to create settlements in the islands and exploit their supposed economic resources led to the introduction of still more alien animals and plants which multiplied the threat to indigenous species.

Centenaries can act as catalytic agents, and the hundredth anniversary of Darwin's brief visit stimulated the first proposals to save the Galapagos from creeping degradation. The Galapagos

Memorial Expedition led by Dr Victor von Hagen in 1935 focused the attention of specialists on the idea that large parts of the archipelago should become nature reserves. The Ecuadorian government passed the first legislation intended to protect wildlife there, and scientists in California, London and New York and conservationists in Ecuador proposed and pressed for the establishment of a research station in the islands, but there was little co-ordination between these groups. When war broke out in 1939 no agency had been set up to implement the Ecuadorian decree and so it was ineffective.

Twenty years later another Darwinian centenary provoked action: the hundredth anniversary of the publication of *The Origin of Species* in 1859. Urged on by the International Zoological Congress, and under the auspices of the United Nations Educational, Scientific and Cultural Organization (UNESCO) and the newly-formed International Union for Conservation of Nature (IUCN), an organising committee was set up under the chairmanship of Sir Julian Huxley, who had been chairman of the London Galapagos Committee in the 1930s. Huxley's name gave great weight, but the main burden of organisation fell on the first president, Professor Victor Van Straelen from Belgium, and his secretary-general Professor Jean Dorst, supported by a distinguished committee, most of whom later achieved international fame in the world of conservation. The majority were scientists from Europe and North America, but this time they and the Ecuadorian conservationists were united in a single international body, the Charles Darwin Foundation for the Galapagos Islands, which was formally constituted under Belgian law in July 1959. Financial help came from individual supporters, and national and international institutions, and virtually all funds were spent on conservation work in the Galapagos as the Foundation maintained no offices or paid staff. Even so, there was never enough money even for the most urgent tasks.

At the same time the government of Ecuador issued another

decree with the same objectives as in 1936: the establishment of a national park and an international scientific station. On the basis of an exploratory survey commissioned by UNESCO and IUCN, a site was chosen at Academy Bay on Santa Cruz Island and during the next four years, roads, a laboratory, a workshop and simple accommodation were built amid the cactus and thorn-scrub. Water and electricity supplies had to be developed, and the lack of local materials and poor communications with the rest of the world made every step hard. The formal inauguration of the Charles Darwin Research Station took place in January 1964 under the blazing equatorial sun. A few days later the basic agreement with the government of Ecuador was signed in Quito, authorising the Foundation to maintain and operate its station until 1989, and to advise the authorities on all scientific and conservation matters affecting the national park.

The visit in 1964 of the Duke of Edinburgh, Honorary Life Member of the Foundation, and his role in the spectacular television film *The Enchanted Isles*, created world-wide interest, and many people wanted to see the islands at first hand. There had always been an implicit understanding that, if the Ecuadorian government would support conservation, the national park might well become the centre of attraction for a tourist industry. As a result of some astute suggestions, a small expert team was sent out in 1965 by the British Ministry of Overseas Development at the request of the government of Ecuador to study this idea. Its report suggested, among much else, that a National Park Service should be established and that visits should take the form of cruises, with tourists sleeping in their ships, thus eliminating the need for onshore accommodation.

Due to a number of factors, including the Darwin legend and an astonishing increase of interest in conservation, tourism developed at a speed that took everyone by surprise. However, the sudden imposition of a tourist industry on an economy dependent on subsistence farming and fishing was bound to raise problems. It was

175

clearly desirable that the sovereign power should assume direct responsibility for the management of the national park, and an Ecuadorian Galapagos National Park Service was set up in 1968 for exactly that purpose. At first it was quartered inside the Darwin station, which helped to establish the close relations between the two bodies that have continued ever since. The first park superintendent was appointed in 1972, since when the National Park Service has increasingly taken charge of operations while the Charles Darwin Foundation continues to provide research and advice.

With the government of Ecuador now very directly involved in the National Park, many uncertainties could be cleared up, including the delicate question of boundaries. In the 1950s the hopes of the most enthusiastic did not rise above saving the uninhabited islands, but the decree establishing the National Park declared that the whole archipelago, apart from land legally acquired before that date, was to be included. Interpretations of this varied widely but, in the end, nearly all the land area was incorporated into the National Park, including large parts of the four inhabited islands; one estimate is as high as 96.6%. Within these boundaries there is no private property and there are no residents. The airfield on Baltra was naturally excluded, but all property and mining rights on James' (Santiago) were extinguished and, to the delight of the conservationists, the whole of this important island, with all its problems, became part of the National Park.

Inevitably there have been clashes of interest. During the dozen years it took to finalise the boundaries squatters moved in, but funds were found to settle them elsewhere. The farmers' cattle wander into the Park and cause serious damage, but of course the settlers cannot suddenly be deprived of their traditional sources of water, salt, wood and sand situated within the Park. Doubtless other problems will arise as the local people, often far too poor to worry about other species, struggle for needs that conflict with conservation. The existence of the National Park and the rapid growth of tourism are bringing about profound changes in an isolated society with a rudimentary social and economic structure. However, these changes have already brought considerable material benefits. The archipelago has been given new status as a separate province and receives greatly increased support from central government. The islands' centuries-old isolation has been ended by the radical transformation of communications with the continent. Tourism is now the main growth industry, and apart from whaling, which merely benefited foreigners, it is by far the most profitable economic enterprise that has been established in the century-and-a-half since the islands were annexed. Together with the associated opportunities in conservation and science, it has conferred advantages on some established residents, and has attracted new immigrants with different backgrounds and outlooks. Successive Ecuadorian governments, working through the National Park Service have collaborated with varying success in schemes to reconcile the divergent interests of tourists, scientists, the armed forces and the local population, which now numbers over 30,000.

The rapid rise in tourist traffic has been a particular cause of concern for ecological reasons to the research station and National Park Service. They were doubtful how far this was compatible with the protection of the unique wildlife upon which the tourism depends. The Park was therefore divided into zones. Vast areas which had remained relatively unchanged ecologically were set aside as 'primitive scientific zones' and no one is allowed in them without good cause and a special permit. A number of sites of outstanding interest to tourists and relatively easy access, 'intensive use zones', were feared to be at risk, so the size of parties allowed on shore at any one time is limited, and all visitors have to follow discreetly marked trails so that they do not disturb nesting seabirds and suckling fur seals or damage the fragile vegetation. No tourist is allowed to remain on shore after sunset, except in specially designated areas, and most importantly, every party has to be accompanied by qualified guides, rigorously trained by the National Park Service and the Darwin station. Visits to any intensive use zone can be suspended if the habitat seems in danger of deterioration, and additional ones have been added over the years.

The conservationists' fears led to prolonged scientific investigation of 'tourist impact'. In order to discover how far, for instance, breeding failures were due to disturbance by visitors and how far to changes in rainfall and ocean currents with consequent effects on the food supply, scientists monitored breeding colonies at various tourist sites and comparable colonies where tourists never set foot. The evidence suggests that, given reasonable limitation on numbers and insistence on good standards of control by qualified guides, visitors will not be a major threat to the existing ecological balance in future.

Some of the damage done in the past proved irreversible; 3.4% of the land of the archipelago had been settled and was not included in the National Park, so there was obviously no chance of restoring these areas to their former condition. Absolute conservation was never feasible. Indeed the objective of official policy since 1972 has been to manage the archipelago as a whole, in which people as well as animals are part of the ecological system. What was achieved was the gradual reduction of human interference in the unoccupied islands and the large parts of the four inhabited islands that had been incorporated into the Park. The slaughter of adult giant tortoises for food, the sale of the young ones as pets and other established customs have been halted, but even these elementary problems were still acute during the early years of the conservation effort.

Human problems still persist but it was found that much more serious threats to the environment arose from the animals and plants that human visitors had successively introduced. In addition to the black rats, there are brown rats, mice, feral goats and donkeys, but more seriously there are numerous invertebrates including fire ants, cottony cushion scale and parasitic flies. In addition there are now more introduced plants in Galapagos than there are native species. Fortunately by no means all of them are found on every island and some islands, such as Fernandina (Narborough) and Genovesa (Tower), have remained entirely free. Nevertheless, the damage that has been and is still being done by introduced animals and plants is enormous, as their alien presence is incompatible with the survival of many of the native species. Only shortly before the Darwin station and the National Park Service were established, fishermen released a number of goats on the island of Pinta (Abingdon) to provide an alternative source of meat on their future visits. The goats proliferated and proceeded to destroy the vegetation with alarming speed. It was necessary to kill upwards of forty thousand during years of exhausting hunting before this devastation could be checked. The vegetation is now recovering but the repeated campaigns imposed a serious drain on manpower and resources. In 2006 with the conclusion of Project Isabela, goats, pigs and donkeys had been eliminated from Northern Isabela and Santiago as well as many of the smaller islands. Staff at the National Park are now equipped with the skills to carry out further eradications on other islands. However alien mammals are much easier to eradicate than the introduced plants and invertebrates so that with many of these species it will be a question of control rather than eradication.

Charles Darwin, deeply impressed like all visitors by the extraordinary tameness of the native species, foresaw 'what havoc the introduction of any beast of prey must cause, before the instincts of the indigenous inhabitants have become adapted to the stranger's craft and power'. Feral dogs prey on the virtually defenceless land and marine iguanas, young tortoises, baby fur-seals, flightless cormorants and penguins. Cats eat the younger iguanas and the birds. Pigs dig out the nests of the tortoises and sea turtles. Rats kill young tortoises and have driven the endemic Galapagos petrel to the verge of extinction.

Partly because of their international fame and importance to science, but more because they were in immediate danger, early priority was given to the protection of the giant tortoises. Originally fourteen or fifteen distinct subspecies had evolved on different islands or on the well-separated volcanoes of Isabela (Albemarle), and of these ten had survived. A single male, christened Lonesome George, of the Pinta Island race was discovered during goat hunting in 1975 but, without a mate, *Geochelone elephantopus abingdoni* could be considered effectively extinct. However there are plans to breed George with closely related tortoises, and to release the closely related Española tortoise on Pinta to help restore the ecosystem. Only three subspecies seemed to be capable of surviving unaided; the rest were endangered in varying degrees and for different reasons. For instance, there was a vigorous breeding stock on Pinzón (Duncan) but the black rats have killed off every hatchling since the 1930s, and although the tortoises are remarkably long-lived, the failure of replacement meant eventual extinction. The experts, lacking the means to control the rats, dug up tortoise eggs and incubated them at the Darwin station in converted bird cages. By trial and error they eventually found methods of rearing the hatchlings. The high degree of success achieved by these methods so impressed the professionals at the San Diego zoo that they funded a more sophisticated rearing house. This made a considerable expansion of the breeding programme possible. The young tortoises are repatriated to their native island as soon as they are big enough to stand up to the rats.

On arid Española (Hood) the situation was even more acute from a different cause. In 1963 the station director, making a rough census of the surviving giant tortoise population, reported: 'Only one tortoise was found on Española in the course of searches by three men for two days. The vegetation of Española has been terribly ravaged by goats: when the tortoise was found it was feeding on a fallen *Opuntia* cactus in competition with fifteen goats.' Later, more survivors were discovered but none under the age of fifty. They were so scattered that apparently they never met, for there was no evidence of breeding in recent decades. So the adults themselves were taken to the research station's pens, where they eventually bred. Their offspring are returned year by year to repopulate their ancestral island, on which the goats have been eradicated and the vegetation is recovering. In this way they have been brought back literally from the brink of extinction.

The Española tortoise and all the other races surviving when the Charles Darwin Foundation was created now seem safe for posterity. Although eight subspecies are bred at the station, they are never crossed and each race is eventually returned to its island of origin. The total of endangered tortoises raised and repatriated in this way now runs into several hundreds. However, it will be a long time before this success story results in a population explosion: giant tortoises live to a great age and do not become sexually mature until they are well into their twenties.

The outcome of this experiment in captive breeding encouraged the scientists to embark on a comparable programme for the huge, endemic land iguanas on Santa Cruz and southern Isabela. A sudden upsurge in the numbers of feral dogs in the 1970s led to their invasion of the iguana breeding colonies on these two islands and the virtual extermination of both populations. The few survivors were taken to the station to breed and large numbers of young ones were successfully raised. Campaigns were mounted to control the wild dogs and then repopulate the original breeding sites with the youngsters, but it may be years before the outcome of this programme is known. Cats, more difficult to eradicate than dogs, certainly prey on young iguanas, and the reintroduction of captive-bred animals to the wild is notoriously full of pitfalls. Fortunately there are populations of land iguanas on other islands which are free from introduced predators.

The Galapagos has fewer species of native mammals than of birds and reptiles. Like the whales, the endemic fur-seals were ruthlessly persecuted for their skins in the last century, and by 1920 they were considered doomed if not actually extinct. However, there were survivors hidden away in remote coves and all they needed in order to prosper was to be left alone. Similarly it did not prove too difficult to discourage the practice of killing the sea-lions to make necklaces from their teeth, and now the population of sea-lions and fur-seals are estimated to be fifty and twenty-five thousand respectively.

The only terrestrial mammals which managed to cross unaided from the mainland and establish themselves in the islands were the little rice rats. They evolved into four new species, but their numbers have been sadly reduced. They have been exterminated on all the islands where black rats have been introduced except Santiago.

The birds have suffered least over the years, in spite of their phenomenal tameness and their slowness in developing any notable instinct of fear. With so high a proportion of species found nowhere else in the world, they were naturally a prime cause of concern, but twenty years of monitoring have shown no general decline. The one exception to this encouraging picture is the splendid, and formerly abundant, Galapagos petrel which is in imminent danger of extinction in the Galapagos. The threat comes not just from introduced rats, but on Santa Cruz the introduced cinchona or quinine tree has invaded the nesting area in the highland and prevents the birds from finding their nesting burrows.

Introduced insects are another pernicious if less visible threat. The most obvious is the fire ant, which is not only unpleasant to humans but is altering the entomological balance in every island where it has established itself. The National Park Service takes drastic action to prevent the spread of this and other species to islands hitherto unaffected.

With the wardens on patrol, the scientists and students living in camps while conducting their researches and the tourists landing for their visits, there is constant danger of inadvertent introduction of alien organisms or their transfer from one island to another. Strict control of food and equipment that may be carried within the

National Park has been largely though not completely successful. The recent introduction of full biosecurity measures, and the spraying of ships and aircraft, will help protect the islands but given the nature of the problem they will only ever be a filter. The only answer is constant vigilance and education of the inhabitants and the visitors.

Equally dangerous is the spread of introduced plants from the farms into the National Park. Guava and cinchona trees are highly valued elsewhere but in the Park they are pests, competing with and endangering the survival of the native species. The National Park Service wardens struggle to eradicate the invading plants while the scientists try to find more effective means of checking their spread. Hitherto there have not been enough resources to bring victory even within sight.

An even lower priority has been given to the protection of the marine resources. This was partly due to the fact that while man's depredations had brought some populations of land animals to the verge of extinction, much of the underwater world of the Galapagos had remained in a virtually pristine condition. A second factor was that no areas of sea had been included in the National Park.

Galapagos had been made one of the first World Heritage Sites in 1978, but the Charles Darwin Foundation always advocated the establishment of a marine zone, if only because so many of the islands' terrestrial species are dependent on the sea for their food. In recent years increasing underwater exploration has led to claims that the marine environment may be just as important as the terrestrial environment. The Galapagos are situated at the confluence of three great Pacific currents – Humboldt, Cromwell and El Niño – and this has resulted in a unique system of marine flora and fauna, with a very high proportion of endemic species. In 1998, after many years of discussion and negotiations, the Ecuadorian Government passed the 'Ley de Regimen Especial para la Conservacion y Desarollo Sustentable de la Provincia de Galapagos' which made the islands a province of Ecuador, a mixed blessing, and reinforced the previously established Instituto Galapagos or INGALA which is charged with implementing the law and development in Galapagos. The INGALA council includes representatives from the National Park and the Charles Darwin Foundation as well as commercial and political representatives. The law regulates movement within the islands and between the islands and the mainland. In addition the government declared the whole of the waters within and around the islands to be a marine reserve. The Galapagos Marine Resources Reserve (GMMR) is the second largest marine reserve in the world and is a World Heritage Site in its own right.

The essential ingredients for ensuring conservation of the Galapagos islands in the future are public interest and international support. Scientists have understood the problem since Darwin's time, although their pessimism led them to concentrate too long on preserving the threatened species in museums. But scientific pressure alone could not have achieved the changes which have been contrived since 1959. The support of scientists and others in the developed world, valuable though it is, is not in itself an adequate motive for Ecuador to wish to conserve the wildlife and ecosystems of its island territory. Understanding and enthusiasm for conservation on the part of the Ecuadorian people as a whole is critical, and this is now beginning to be won on a wider scale.

Television has done most to bring the Galapagos and its fantastic wildlife into the homes of millions, both in Ecuador and throughout the world. Another important development was the scheme whereby the Darwin station gave scholarships to undergraduates and postgraduates from Ecuadorian universities. They were usually attached as assistants to senior visiting scientists, and thus acquired experience in field research for which there was otherwise little opportunity in Ecuador. This caught on and, as the training of scientists and technologists was an essential part of the national development plan, the government requested a big expansion of the programme. The Charles Darwin Foundation could not afford this so the government offered to meet the cost. This had various consequences: Ecuador became much the largest contributor to the research station's budget; links with the national universities were expanded and strengthened; and the station could engage an adequate number of highly qualified scientists. This co-operation in research in the Galapagos, which previously had been the virtual monopoly of foreigners, promises well for both the Darwin Foundation and the Ecuadorian scientific establishment. Similarly, the tourists who flocked to the islands were at first mainly from Europe and North America, but more recently Ecuadorians have been arriving in their hundreds, and are getting to know and appreciate their own archipelago.

That so much was achieved in the Galapagos is an abiding tribute to the sympathetic understanding of successive governments and the pride of Ecuador in its island possession. What may well be the world's most important archipelago from the point of view of evolutionary science was saved for posterity. At the same time, an offshore province which was a drain on the nation became an economic asset. These diverse achievements were brought about by a peculiar alliance of national government and international science.

In recent years the cause of environmental conservation and the urge to subdue and exploit nature have not been easy to reconcile, particularly its fishing industry, and there have been a number of conflicts. This, combined with immigration problems, uncontrolled growth in the tourism industry and the serious threat posed by invasive species led to the World Heritage Committee declaring Galapagos a World Heritage Site in Danger in 2007. This had the effect of waking the Ecuadorian Government to the many problems in the islands and steps are being taken to resolve some of the problems. This serves to emphasise the need for constant effort to ensure that the islands remain the natural laboratory that so inspired Charles Darwin.

17

The Human Element

T HIS IS THE HISTORY of the human experience in the Galapagos, and not only their natural history. After the Incas came Tomás de Berlanga; and after him a colourful procession of buccaneers and explorers, sailors and scientists, pioneers and convicts. In the century following the annexation of the islands by Ecuador, permanent settlements began to be established, slowly and painfully, but their existence was always precarious. How have they fared in the last fifty years?

As we have seen, most of the early settlers came to the islands involuntarily. The first willing volunteers were the Europeans who arrived from Norway and Germany in the 1920s. However, they too had great difficulty in creating viable lives for themselves and the majority sooner or later failed and returned to Europe. After the tragic Charles' Island disasters, only the Wittmer family, outstanding survivors, continued to live there. However, some of the Norwegians who had come originally to Charles' (Floreana) moved later to Santa Cruz and started farming in the highlands above Academy Bay, near the village of Bellavista. They were joined later by other immigrants, mainly from Germany, and Santa Cruz became, as it still is, the main centre for settlement. For the most part these were not romantic idealists but simply people attracted by the lifestyle of the islands and disillusioned by the mounting problems they knew in Europe. This little group continued their hard-working life as producers of coffee, bananas and sugar cane until the war came.

After 1942 and the construction of the US Air Force base on Baltra, the settlers for the first time had the opportunity to earn money and enjoy a standard of living higher than they could get by subsistence farming. Before then it was only on the Cobos sugar plantations on San Cristobal and the Gil coffee plantations on Isabela that agriculture had been developed on a commercial basis with cash crops. From 1942 there were other possibilities for the enterprising. Some of the islanders got jobs at the base; others, such as Christian Stampa, caught fish and lobster to sell to the US Air Force.

In 1948–49, with the money he had earned working for the base, Stampa left for Norway with the idea of bringing back a group of Norwegians to join those already on the islands. He managed to attract enough people, bought a boat and set off for Galapagos, but she was tragically wrecked near Vigo on New Year's Eve, 1949, with the loss of all aboard save one small girl. The Norwegian colonists never recovered from this blow and over the years they gradually drifted back to Norway so that now none remain. Other islanders were able slowly to improve the efficiency of their farming and, in due course, some of them began to exploit the rich fishing potential (particularly of bacalao) more systematically than before. Gradually the economy and social framework of the islands developed attracting more people both from Ecuador and from Europe and the rest of the Americas. Communications improved and eventually a regular monthly service by boat from Guayaquil was established.

These developments naturally came in stages. After World War II a number of new European settlers arrived. Later, in 1959–60, there was an attempt to establish an American colony on San Cristobal. The plan was to grow coffee on a large scale on a co-operative basis, and around one hundred Americans were originally involved. Sadly the project was short-lived, and within a year all but two families had returned home. However, the project stimulated the Ecuadorian authorities to encourage their own nationals to colonise the islands and a more organised attempt was made to divide up suitable land for distribution to new colonists. In the late sixties further encouragement brought out a number of farmers from the Province of Loja in southern Ecuador; but it was not until the tourist industry and communications with the mainland started to develop in earnest that the population increases became significant.

The establishment of the Darwin Station and the National Park Service and, even more notably the growth of the tourist industry, have certainly done most to stimulate the economy of the Galapagos – and of course to change the old island way of life. Since its foundation twenty years ago, the Darwin Station has grown steadily and played a large part in the development of Santa Cruz as the commercial centre of the archipelago, while San Cristobal remains the administrative capital, presided over by the Governor, and the headquarters of the Second Naval Zone of the Ecuadorian Navy.

In recent years the main reason for outside interest in the Galapagos is, of course, the intense and growing desire of foreign visitors, in the first place North Americans and Europeans from over-populated cities, to enjoy holidays which take them back to the natural world and, in the case of the more imaginative, to the origins of the human species itself. However, for the tourist industry to flourish, or even to start on a serious scale, transport, both to and among the islands, was vital. They were first made more accessible to tourists by the establishment of an improved shipping service by the supply ship *Cristobal Carrier* which, from the early 1960s, brought some passengers on each of her freight runs. The *Carrier*, as she was affectionately known, was a converted freighter with an extra 'top deck' added. This was 'Tourist Class' but it was definitely superior to First Class on the main deck. She made a regular run calling at San Cristobal, Santa Cruz, Floreana and

Isabela before returning to pick up cattle in Santa Cruz to be taken back to the mainland. When she had a group of tourists on board she would pick up a guide in San Cristobal and stop at South Plaza or Sante Fé for the tourists. For a period between 1962 and 1965 she also called at Santiago Island to collect salt which was being extracted from a lake in a cinder cone close to the shore. (This enterprise failed when the price of salt dropped.)

In 1968 a three-masted schooner, the *Golden Cachalot*, arrived from England and began to offer the first-ever tourist cruises in the archipelago. In the same year the Ecuadorian Air Force resurfaced the main runway of the Baltra airstrip and more frequent flights (but not yet a regular service) to and from the mainland became possible.

In 1970 the first major tourism venture in the islands started with the sixty-passenger cruise ship *Lina A* under charter to Metropolitan Touring of Quito. This ship made regular three- and four-day cruises around the islands and, with the accompanying twice weekly flights, made them easily accessible for the first time to anyone with the necessary means. This accessibility also enabled private yacht owners to operate more successfully and a growing number of small yachts and converted fishing vessels started cruising in the islands carrying between four and ten passengers. Today there are around one hundred small vessels offering a wide variety of comfort and convenience to the visitor. The number of cruise ships has also grown to ten, all limited by the National Park Service to a maximum of ninety passengers and with their itineraries carefully controlled. This increase in tourism, apart from its overall impact on the economy of the islands, has made Santa Cruz increasingly the centre of the tourist industry because of its central location and the road, built in 1971–73, to link the village and port of Puerto Ayora to Baltra where the airport is located.

The permanent population of the islands has naturally increased in step with their economic development. In 1950 there were only 1,346 people of whom 250 were on Santa Cruz; by 1962 the population had grown to 2,301 with some 550 on Santa Cruz, and by 1974 the totals were 4,277 with 1,100 on Santa Cruz. Today the population of the islands is over 30,000 with Santa Cruz having over 20,000 inhabitants.

Tourism has long overtaken agriculture as the mainstay of the Galapagos economy. Agriculture has been most successful where it was first established in Santa Cruz, San Cristobal and Isabela. These and other islands have very dry coastal plains, but above about 200 metres on the southern slopes of these islands there is an extensive moist zone. The land is fertile though rocky in places and, once the native trees and bushes are cleared, provides good pasture and will easily produce bananas, coffee, avocados, papayas, pineapples and a variety of European vegetables – subject to the depredations of the local animal and insect populations.

From the early 1960s, as the shipping connection to Guayaquil became more regular, the cattle industry also developed. Farmers had always had to contend with the wild cattle which roamed the islands, but these were gradually either domesticated or shot for food. As the cattle exports developed new blood was brought in and the quality of the animals gradually improved. For a while cattle farming brought prosperity to farmers, but with the fall of the Argentine *peso* in the 1990s it became uneconomic to ship cattle to the mainland and so coffee remains the only significant agricultural export and the focus of the farming sector is more on supplying local markets. This has had a negative impact on land in the farming zone as less land is now cultivated and invasive weed species have taken over many previously farmed areas.

Fishing, which once was the main economic activity, burgeoned with the development of the sea cucumber fishery in the 1980s and 90s, but with the demise of that industry due to serious overfishing, and the recent clampdown on the shark-fin fishery, the sector is no longer a major contributor to the economy. The National Park has, however, just started to allow tourists on artisanal fishing boats and to license sports fishing under a carefully controlled regime.

A group of oceanic islands which belongs to a continental country will necessarily have its special economic interests and needs and yet may not have the political strength to ensure that it is not treated as though it were just another 'part of the continent'. As the Galapagos developed during the seventies, it became apparent that some organisation was required to help coordinate development and to co-operate with the National Park Service to ensure that the development was compatible with the National Park's conservation philosophy and plans. In 1980 the Instituto Nacionál de Galápagos (INGALA) was set up with the object of assisting the economic development and standard of living of the islanders within the framework of the National Park, and taking account of the need to preserve as far as possible the unique ecosystem of the archipelago. In the few years since it was established INGALA has become an important element of life in Galapagos; their main works have been in improving communications and standards of farming and introducing new techniques. They have constructed new airport terminals at Baltra and San Cristobal and they have provided additional doctors and dentists free of charge for the people of the islands. INGALA works always with the municipal authorities and with the National Park Service and the Darwin Station to ensure that their development projects are in the interests both of the national environment and of the human inhabitants.

If the human history of the Galapagos were only the story of man's struggle to survive, it would nevertheless be a vivid example of the principle which Charles Darwin first observed at work there in the animal world. However, the history shows more than that, as any visitor to the Galapagos Islands can learn directly by seeing them today. The lesson to be learned concerns the relationship between man and the natural world. There, man is the alien, and the animals, the birds, even the vegetation, belong more truly in them than the most adaptable of humans.

To discover the Galapagos we must come in a humble spirit, not to dominate the environment, nor exploit its resources, not to regulate the natural creation but to find a niche in it for ourselves. Other islands can be dominated by men and have been used for all kinds of ends. Some are utterly barren and beyond our reach. But the Galapagos world is neither of these. Here there is a balance of nature which existed without man once and exists now without the fear of man. There are no doubt other places in which human beings can live side by side and in the same dimension as the animal creation, but few where we can experience so complete a revelation of nature. In the Galapagos, as in few other places left to us, the animals are in a state of innocence living in a true wilderness. So long as men came to govern, to exploit and to impose themselves on that small and special world, they were at cross-purposes with the natural order and its various inhabitants. It would be easy enough now to use our superior technology to force the Galapagos environment to conform to human needs. But how much better to repair the damage of the human impact and to preserve this wilderness in which all creatures have their place: to make it again as the Garden of Eden was when Adam and Eve first walked there.

Appendix:
The Wildlife of the Galapagos

THE TORTOISES

The tortoise (galapagos in Spanish) are the symbol of the Galapagos Islands. It was the multitudes of these huge beasts that impressed the Bishop of Panama and the buccaneers, and that attracted the whalers and the collectors; today it is only the more energetic visitor who can hope to see one in the wild. According to tradition it was once possible to walk without touching the ground by stepping from the back of one tortoise to another. Now most of the survivors can be found only in remoter parts of the islands to which access is difficult. Perhaps we ought to be thankful that it requires such an arduous trek to reach their last refuges because, if it were not so, they would all have become extinct some time ago.

When their precursors reached the islands they found it a veritable paradise. They had no competitors for food except the herbivorous land iguanas, and no serious enemies at all. The only hazard they faced were those of climate and terrain. Over the centuries there must have been periods of unusually intense drought which would drastically reduce the food supply but, like the cactus on which it feeds, the tortoise has an extraordinary inherent resistance to such conditions and can stay alive for many months without food or water. The rugged terrain presented its peculiar problems; there was always the possibility of falling into a steepsided lava hole or becoming wedged in a crevice but, for the slow, lumbering reptiles born to this savage land, such dangers were not too great. From time to time, volcanic eruptions must have taken their toll. In 1901 Rollo Beck, when collecting specimens on one of the Isabela volcanoes, noticed that almost all the old tortoises living around the summit had shells which were irregularly scarred and pitted, whereas the old ones living near the foot of the mountain had smooth shells, as had the younger ones in both areas. The only explanation he could think of was that, at some time in the past, those near the top might have been showered with burning volcanic cinders. There were several craters close to where the scarred tortoises lived but none which appeared to have erupted at all recently. So, if Beck's very tentative suggestion is correct, the big tortoises must have been very old indeed.

The great age of the tortoises has always fascinated humans, and for the Chinese they are the symbol of longevity. There are reports of them reaching the age of one hundred and fifty years. No method has yet been discovered of determining the age of the venerable patriarchs by studying their shells. For the first ten or twenty years the carapaces of the younger tortoises put on annual growth rings, as trees do, but after that it is no longer possible to trace them owing to abrasion of the surface. If the giant tortoise can be saved from extinction, our great-great grandchildren should have some definite information, because the Charles Darwin Research Station is now marking the shells so that the tortoises will be individually identifiable. Meanwhile, lacking scientific proof, we are entitled to regard these seemingly antique creatures as being at least as old as they look.

As is natural for a creature so long-lived, the giant tortoise has tremendous powers of endurance. Even when death comes to claim one of the senior citizens, a long time may pass before it yields. Miguel Castro, who was brought up on the islands and served as the first conservation officer of the Darwin station, knows the tortoises more intimately than most. He says that when an ancient one reaches the point where it no longer has the strength to search for food, it lies down and remains in the same spot for months, completely immobile, until death finally overtakes it.

It is not necessary to discuss here whether the various kinds of tortoises in the archipelago should be classified as separate species or as subspecies. For practical purposes we can say that there were originally fifteen races in the Galapagos, falling into two main classes. First, there are those with relatively short necks and high, dome-shaped carapaces, which curve downwards, coming low over both head and tail. Then there are those with very long necks, and carapaces which are rather flat on top but tilted up in front, like old-fashioned Spanish saddles. The dome-shaped races are found on Santa Cruz, and on some of the Albemarle volcanoes. These islands have upland areas with plenty of moisture and the lushest vegetation in the archipelago, so that the tortoises can graze at ground level. The saddle-backed races belong to arid areas such as Española and Pinzon Islands and the northern volcano of Isabela, where there is no grass for most of the time and so the tortoises have to stretch upwards to get at the cactus and the scanty foliage of the bushes. It is an obvious advantage in these conditions to have a long neck and a shell canted upwards in front.

The biggest tortoises are to be found in the humid, cloud-swathed mountain zones. Beck tells of capturing one which needed twelve men to carry it down to the coast. There are periods of drought in the uplands but the supply of food and water is generally much more abundant. Where they can find it, the tortoises love fresh water, a fact which much impressed Darwin. Where it can find a pool it will lie all night half-submerged in the shallows, or failing a pool it will make use of a damp spot, churning up the soil until it has made itself a mudhole in which it can gratefully wallow. Buoyed up by the water, the tortoise can take some of its enormous weight off its feet, breathe more freely and make good the oxygen deficiency which it has incurred during the exertion of travelling or feeding. For this elephantine creature movement must be laborious, so whenever possible it takes its ease, like its water, in great gulps and does not move again until it has to.

Although a specialist in slow motion, the tortoise is capable of short bursts of what, to it, must seem like speed – for instance, in pursuit of a female. On these occasions it also finds its voice. Herman Melville wrote that the special characteristic of the Galapagos was that 'no voice, no howl is heard; the chief sound of life here is a hiss'. While this is an admirable generalisation strikingly expressed, there is an exception to it; during the act of mating, but at no other time, the male tortoise gives vent to loud grunts and roars, which can be heard nearly 400 metres away. Otherwise Melville is correct, for the tortoise breathes by gulping air into its lungs under pressure and then letting it out again with a long, soft hiss. The female never roars, whatever the provocation.

On the cloud-capped volcanoes, where there is usually water in the higher reaches, there is a great deal of migration, and smooth trails have been worn in the lava by the passing of countless generations of tortoises. The frequency and the motivation for these migrations need further study, but one reason for leaving the lush, wet pastures for the arid, lower slopes seems clear – the females like to lay their eggs in the hot, dry earth where the chances of successful incubation are better. To achieve this they must often travel several kilometres over difficult ground. Darwin calculated that on these treks they can do about six kilometres a day. Having found a suitable spot, the tortoise scoops out a hole with her hind legs, moistening the soil by urinating. She then lays her round, white eggs, often in layers separated by a thin coat of earth, and then fills the hole. The damp soil dries in the hot sun to form a hard cap. The value of this sealing process is obscure from the point of view of survival because, unless there is rain to soften the soil again, some of the newly-hatched young are unable to break through the cap. Given the long life of tortoises, the number of eggs in a clutch (usually between five and twelve), the fact that a female may lay several clutches in a year, and the absence of enemies, this would not have been much of a handicap to survival in the past. However, with all the new hazards introduced by humans, it is now a factor of some significance.

On the smaller islands without heights to attract moisture, the tortoises have a much harder time, and they never reach the enormous size of those on the high, humid slopes. Except at long and irregular intervals they drink no water, and there is little herbage on which to graze. Yet they were numerous enough when the islands were discovered. They found adequate food in the pads and fallen trunks of the cacti together with any foliage, and could browse on the desiccated shrubs. From this spartan diet they were also able to derive enough liquid to sustain life. Now on some islands, they have to compete for food with the introduced goats and, unlike their fellows on the larger islands, they have no moist pastures to which they can retreat.

Of the original fourteen or fifteen races of tortoises in the archipelago, there were no less than five on Isabela, one on each of the five great volcanoes. The volcanoes were sufficiently isolated from one another to allow a different race to evolve on each, and survivors of all five races still exist. Each of the other ten races was found on a separate island. The race on Floreana Island was hunted to extinction over a century ago. Floreana was a favourite haunt of pirates and whalers, who took their toll, but the tortoises were still fairly numerous when the first disastrous settlement was established in 1832. Only a few years later, there were neither tortoises nor men on the island. The tortoises on two of the smaller islands, Santa Fé and Rabida, may have survived a little longer but they, in their turn, were exterminated. As numbers dropped rapidly in all the islands it became more and more difficult and less and less profitable to hunt them on the grand scale, and so the remnants of the other tortoise populations lingered on. Only one race has apparently been

Galapagos

Galapagos

irretrievably doomed in our time; this is the Pinta tortoise. Owing to slaughter by fishermen before the establishment of the Darwin station, only a solitary male is known to survive known as Lonesome George and, as all efforts to find a female have failed it seems that he will be the last of his kind.

The Fernandina tortoise is something of a mystery. It is known to scientists as *Geochelone elephantopus phantastica* and no doubt merits every word of its name, but particularly the last, because only one specimen has ever been recorded. An old male was collected in 1906 by Rollo Beck and now resides in solitary state in the museum of the California Academy of Sciences. Otherwise the race remains an enigma. In recent years the Darwin research station has made several expeditions up this vast and formidable volcano in the hope of finding further specimens. Roger Perry, when director of the station, made a particularly thorough search, as did that indefatigable mountaineer, Eric Shipton. Not a trace was found, though there is still a faint possibility that survivors may exist in some oasis in this wilderness of lava. Perhaps the race was wiped out by one of the frequent eruptions of this still very active volcano. For once man does not seem to have been to blame.

There are around fifteen thousand tortoises in Galapagos, the two largest populations are those on Volcan Alcedo on Isabela Island where there are some five thousand individuals, and on Santa Cruz with a population of around three thousand. There are significant populations on both of the southern volcanoes on Isabela, though poaching and volcanic eruptions are a constant threat. The populations in Northern Isabela are in reasonable shape and on Santiago and Española they are increasing following the eradication of goats, and on Santiago pigs. The problem of rats on Pinzon has not yet been solved, so that population is still endangered.

IGUANAS

Of all the creatures on the Galapagos, none fits into the fantastic landscape more aptly than the iguana – both islands and beasts are 'out of this world'. If parts of the archipelago seem to resemble the moon, the iguanas are like something out of science fiction. There are two species, one living in the arid zones and the other exclusively along the shore-line. They may be descended from a single ancestral stock that reached the islands long ago, but they have diverged so far that they no longer look alike and their habits are utterly different.

The land iguanas are not altogether unlike their relatives on the mainland, but they have evolved along different lines, and also vary from island to island. Some populations are predominantly reddish brown and grey, while others more brightly pigmented in a range of shades running from vivid yellow through orange to dark brown. The adults are about a metre long and weigh about thirteen kilograms. With a crest of spines like a row of long, pointed teeth running down their backs, they look very fierce but are, in fact, mild creatures and will not bite unless molested. Their powerful jaws serve for crushing the cactus pads and fruits, which they swallow without chewing together with a good proportion of the steel-hard spines, though they may remove some of these with their feet. The land iguanas are lethargic creatures, passing much of their lives in a torpid state, but if frightened they can change their usual undignified gait into an even more laughable waddling burst of speed. They can also climb trees to get at whatever foliage there is, but here again, their movements are not much livelier than those of a sloth. They dig shallow burrows between the slabs of lava or preferably in the soft volcanic tuff to which they retire at night, or when disturbed, or to lay their large, elongated eggs.

It has been their misfortune that despite their appearance, so repulsive to many people, their white flesh is considered a delicacy. On James' Island (Santiago), where Darwin had difficulty in finding a place to pitch his tent as all the suitable spots had been so thoroughly tunnelled by these great lizards, there are now no land iguanas. Populations everywhere have been reduced or eliminated by men and dogs eating them, or by goats and donkeys pre-empting their food supply. Where they are left free from interference, their powers of survival seem tremendous. Within twenty months of the violent eruption of the great Narborough volcano in 1968 the land iguanas were already repopulating the main crater.

If the land iguana, with its bold splashes of colour, is the gaudiest of the archipelago's reptilian inhabitants, the marine iguana, except the larger adult males, can lay strong claim to being the drabbest. Like the sea-fringed lava on which it spends its life, it is shiny black when wet, dark grey when dry. This gives it wonderful camouflage but what advantage this confers is obscure since, until the arrival of man, it had virtually no enemies on land to hide from. As it is cold-blooded and lacks the automatic thermostat of warm-blooded animals, it may be that its black hide is useful in absorbing more rapidly the heat of the sun after a long immersion in the sea. Darwin described it as 'a hideous-looking creature, stupid, and sluggish in its movements', but he could not resist its fascination and devoted some of his very best pages to describing it.

Whatever its ancestry, the marine iguana is radically different not only from the Galapagos land iguana but from all other lizards in the world. It is the only sea-going lizard, and lives exclusively on seaweed, which it browses either on the tidal rocks or below water. Scuba divers say they have found it at depths of up to ten metres. It swims gracefully by undulating its body and its long, flat-sided tail. The feet, which are not webbed, hang loosely and are not used for swimming, but their powerful talons are admirably adapted to climbing and clinging on the slippery rocks. While the land iguana has adapted to these arid volcanoes by contriving to get sufficient water from the cacti, the marine iguana has so adapted that it can process the seawater it swallows with the algae it feeds on. It absorbs far more salt than its body requires, but it has desalination glands in its head. At intervals it ejects a highly concentrated saline solution through its nostrils in the form of a fine spray, which makes it look even more like the legendary fire-breathing dragon.

Its fiery appearance is belied by its harmless behaviour, as Captain Porter, of the US Navy tells us when describing his first encounter:

> In some spots a half acre of ground would be so completely covered with them as to appear as though it was impossible for another to get in the space; they would all keep their eyes fixed constantly on us, and we at first supposed they prepared to attack us. We soon, however, discovered them to be the most timid of animals, and in a few moments knocked down hundreds of them with our clubs, some of which we brought on board and found to be excellent eating, and many preferred them greatly to the turtle.

Porter, like so many other mariners, had his 'fun' which did the marine iguana population no good. Fortunately for this species, his estimation of its culinary qualities was not shared by everyone. It is alleged that there is little meat on them apart from the tail, and they do look rather nauseating to the more sensitive gourmet. In any event, the sport of iguana-bashing lost its popular appeal as the years went by.

The marine iguanas are still quite numerous and widespread in the Galapagos. Small groups or large herds are to be found on most islands, even the lesser ones. They can still be seen sunning themselves on the black rocks, packed side by side like sardines in a can, but all facing in the same direction. They seem to congregate, not in family parties but in age groups, all much the same size. Their whole life is spent along the shore-line. They rarely venture more than 10 metres inland and there is nothing to show that they ever go to sea at all except to feed.

Their ability to swim may be responsible for the small degree of divergence between the races on the different islands; some may have been carried from one island to another, resulting in cross-breeding. To the casual observer there is no difference, except in the case of adult males. These big fellows sometimes exceed 1.2 metres in length and weigh over 9 kilograms. Instead of being a uniform dirty black, these monsters are a patchwork of striking colours, which vary from island to island.

SEA-LIONS AND SEALS

Sea-lions and seals have a potent magic for human beings, for although they must keep to their own element, the sea, they seem happy to share most of their activities with us if we can reach them. We all succumb to their charm in greater or lesser degrees, for example, the engaging sight of the females suckling their babies on the beach, or the young sea-lions at play, chasing one another under the pellucid water, tumbling on the sand or playing 'king of the castle', as one tries to knock the other off the top of a boulder. Sea-lions have not always been such popular favourites. Even now, when we know so much more about their habits and disposition, it is disconcerting, to say the least, to be charged for the first time by a half-ton bull sea-lion. It travels through the water like a torpedo and, instead of stopping at the water's edge, rushes up the beach, ponderously, but with a turn of speed that one would not expect from a creature with flippers instead of legs. Roaring and showing his fine, big teeth, he can strike fear into the hearts of the boldest. That doughty sailor, Captain Woodes Rogers, the most successful privateer of his generation, who was always ready to board an enemy ship or lead the attack on a town relates:

A very large one made at me, several times, and had I not happened to have a Pike-staff pointed with Iron in my Hand, I might have been killed by him; (one of our Men having narrowly escap'd the Day before). I was on the level Sand when he came open-mouth'd at me out of the Water, as quick and fierce as the most angry Dog let loose. I struck the point into his Breast and wounded him all the three times he made at me, which forced him at last to retire with an ugly Noise, snarling and showing his long Teeth at me out of the water. This amphibious Beast was as big as a large Bear.

With all deference to the bold buccaneer, he was stretching credibility. The history of the Galapagos Islands is full of blood and violent death, but the most painstaking research has failed to disclose a single case of a man being killed by a sea-lion though the reverse used to be common enough.

The bull sea-lion rarely bites a human, but it frequently bites and is bitten by other bulls. Fights to the death, if they occur at all, must be abnormal, but fighting for dominance is part of the bull's way of life. As with many other gregarious animals, the bull sea-lion only maintains his mastery of the herd by contest. There are far more adult males than there are herds, and the majority of the bulls are relegated to monastic seclusion on the less desirable sections of the shore. They naturally resent this and constantly try to depose the reigning monarch and take over his harem. The price of sovereignty is eternal vigilance and the master bull must be on guard day and night. For much of the time he patrols the sea frontier of his territory, in a series of shallow dives, punctuated by hearty roars. This patrolling has a useful function, apart from defending his seignorial rights, because he chivvies back any youngster that may venture out too far, where it would run the very real risk of being attacked by a shark.

However, patrolling is an arduous existence and leaves little time for feeding, if the bulls feed at all during the mating season. According to Dr Bryan Nelson's detailed observations on the beach where he studied sea-lions for months, no bull kept it up without interruption for more than a few weeks. Either he got too hungry, was worn out by his conjugal duties, or possibly grew bored with the never-ending sentry duty. Whatever the reason, the master would disappear for a time and another bull would take over the harem and fight off new challenges until he was replaced in turn. The females seemed to accept whatever master the fortunes of battle sent them, continuing unperturbed their leisurely existence wallowing in the dry sand, scratching themselves, and above all sleeping. So the harem system is not quite as inequitable as it would appear to anyone studying it over a short period; given enterprise, perseverance and a fighting spirit, every bull can have his day.

The Galapagos sea-lion does not belong to the same species as the other South American sea-lions, which live well to the south in much colder waters. However, it does have two close relatives which are widely separated geographically, one form being found in the Sea of Japan and the other along the coast of California. All the circus sea-lions belong to this intelligent species. Naturally they are at their best in the water, where they can display their grace and skill, but even on land they are not without their clumsy charm. Emerging from the water their short velvety hair is nearly jet black but, as they dry in the sun, they become lighter and lighter, changing to a pale gold. Though some of us may admire the sea-lion's skin, it has always been despised by the fur trade, which explains why Galapagos sea-lions are still there in large numbers to give pleasure to all beholders. In the past some were brutally and inefficiently killed for their teeth in order to make necklaces for visitors, but since the organisation of the National Park Service, this practice has stopped.

Fur-seals once abounded in the Galapagos. It is one of the many oddities of the islands that fur seals should live and breed right on the equator. In all probability they made their way north in the cool waters of the Humboldt current and gradually adapted to the local conditions. There was plenty of food, and caves and overhangs where they could escape the worst of the sun's heat, while the water temperature was lower than elsewhere on the equator. Somehow they contrived to overcome the natural difficulties and prospered to become the largest tropical colony of the southern hemisphere genus. Then man came. The sealers and often whalers and fishermen, when opportunity offered, took their toll. There is no reliable estimate of the thousands that were killed in the nineteenth century, but in 1898–9 the sealing schooner *Julia E. Whaler* collected only two hundred and forty-four skins; the numbers were so depleted that hunting was no longer profitable and this was the last big commercial venture. During their twelve-month stay, the *Academy* expedition found only one seal and in 1930 Dr Townsend wrote: 'The peculiar fur-seal of the Galapagos, although formerly abundant, is probably near extinction as none have been seen during recent years.'

Nobody would have been more pleased than Dr Townsend to know that events have belied his dismal prophecy. He came at the worst moment of all, when scientists thought that the Galapagos fauna was doomed and that the best thing they could do was to collect as much as possible of the little that remained and preserve it for posterity in museums. Since then the Ecuadorian Government's prohibition of all killing and trading (better observed in the case of seals than most prohibitions) and the patrolling of the islands by the Park Service and the Darwin station, have radically changed the situation. The latest survey estimated the seal population at twenty-five thousand, while there are some fifty-thousand sea-lions.

Not unnaturally after such persecution, the fur-seals tend to live in remote places, where landing is tricky or impossible, and are still, though decreasingly, shy of humans, at least on land. But that novel phenomenon, man in the water, is not recognised as an enemy and, while they have more inhibitions than sea-lions, they will play joyously with people in the sea. Perhaps it is because they know that we are clearly the inferior species in water.

BIRDS

The giant tortoises and iguanas have attracted most attention from the human visitors, perhaps because of their great size, but the Galapagos birds are at least as fascinating and are far more numerous. Although oceanic islands never have as wide a range of species as continents, the Galapagos are better endowed than most, partly because divergence of common stocks has produced different species on individual islands. It is considered today that there are sixty breeding species, of which thirty-six are found nowhere else, while a good many others are distinct subspecies confined to the Galapagos. In addition some sixty species of regular migrants and occasional visitors were recorded at the latest count.

Bird-watchers who visit the Galapagos, particularly during the northern winter, will recognise a number of old friends. As they sail through the islands they can see flocks of red and northern phalaropes (in Britain confusingly known as grey and red-necked phalaropes). In and around the lagoons there are various familiar plovers, sandpipers, turnstones, willets, stilts, oystercatchers, dowitchers, sanderlings, wandering tatlers from Alaska and blue-winged teal. There are four breeding herons, which differ little from the northern races of the great blue heron, yellow-crowned night heron, green heron and American egret. This last will also be familiar to Europeans under the name of great white egret, as will the short-eared and barn owls.

The Galapagos pintail, a very distinct subspecies of the Bahama pintail, is found in good numbers; odd though it may seem, its favourite breeding place is the lake in the crater of Narborough volcano to which it returns whenever that turbulent mountain's eruptions permit. In most upland areas there is a relative of the little continental black rail. More widely spread, there are two flycatchers, one closely related to the continental vermillion flycatcher, and the other belonging to the same genus as the great crested flycatcher, though smaller in size. There is also a local variety of the yellow warbler, distinct from the continental races but readily recognisable.

The swallow family is represented by the Galapagos martin, which nests in crevices in the lava cliffs.

In the seas round the islands you will find the shearwaters and petrels, flitting and gliding over the waves with stiff-winged mastery. The Galapagos shearwater nests in cracks and tunnels in the lava, and no less than four species of storm petrel breed on the islands. The nesting area of Elliot's storm petrel has not yet been discovered but, as the Galapagoan race is present throughout the year and is found nowhere else, there is no reasonable doubt that it breeds somewhere in the islands, possibly on the Roca Redonda. The Madeiran storm petrel is often to be seen feeding by day on fish and cephalopods. It nests in slight hollows in the soil or inside small caves.

Two species of petrel are of particular interest to ornithologists for very different reasons. On uninhabited Genovesa Island, there is a huge and thriving colony of the Galapagos storm petrel. Although they are nocturnal feeders, day after day, from dawn until dusk, thousands of these tiny seabirds flutter around the sky above Genovesa Island like dense clouds of gnats, each of them banking, twisting and diving on their individual course and occasionally colliding with a dull thud. Nobody has yet been able to provide a reasonable explanation for this curious behaviour, and it is one of the most notable ornithological sights of the Galapagos. If this prolonged communal flitting is carried out by successive relays of different birds, the total population must be immense, up to a quarter of a million breeding pairs.

In contrast, the Galapagos petrel is under threat of total extermination. As a breeding species it is restricted to the Galapagos, and until relatively recently it was safe enough in the islands, where it nests in burrows and caves above the 150 metre line, in areas more or less permanently shrouded in mist during the breeding season. The substantial colony on Santa Cruz came under threat after the tragic failure of the Norwegian attempt to settle on the island. The settlers perished or left, but the pigs they introduced multiplied rapidly. The pigs included nesting petrels in their diet to such an extent that, during the breeding season, their flesh was so tainted by the taste and smell of petrels as to be virtually inedible. While pigs and dogs are no longer a threat, the rapid spread of the introduced cinchona or quinine tree is threatening the nesting habitat of this endemic species.

The sea-birds must have been the first to establish themselves on the islands because there was fish for them to feed on, before the vegetation and insects needed to support a population of land birds appeared. While the great distinction of the Galapagos is that a high proportion of its birds and beasts exist nowhere else, there is a small number of species of more-widely-distributed seabirds that have colonised the islands, which are no less interesting because they are to be found on other tropical shores. The brown pelican is a constant source of delight; however clumsy-looking it may appear, it is a very efficient operator both in the air and in the water. The brown noddy, which nests on ledges and in cavities in the sea cliffs, resembles a photographic negative of a tern, with its dark body and pale cap, but has a rounded instead of a forked tail. Another cliff-dweller is a bird of quite exceptional beauty, the red-billed tropic bird. It is particularly attractive in flight, with the rapid beat of its white, finely-barred wings and its incredibly long, slender tailfeathers streaming out behind.

The archipelago is fortunate to have two out of the world's five species of frigate (or man-o'-war) birds breeding there. Their ranges within the islands overlap to a small extent, and although the two species are quite distinct to the scientist, the newcomer may find it difficult to distinguish between the adult males, except at very close quarters. Unfortunately, they spend much of their day soaring around effortlessly at inconveniently great heights for the observer. The juveniles with their white heads, dark breasts and white bellies are also virtually identical. Although the females of both species have white breasts, the great frigate has a whitish throat and foreneck, while these parts are blackish in the magnificent frigate. Both species are supremely well-designed flying machines.

They have a higher ratio of wing area to weight than any other bird; with a wing span of up to 2.4 metres, their bones weigh a mere 110 grams. This phenomenal aerodynamic specialisation has been achieved at the expense of other qualities, and their small legs and feet will not serve either for walking or swimming. Their plumage is not fully waterproof so they rarely alight on the sea, but they can pick up a fish or a squid from the surface or from a fisherman's net without even touching the water. Fishing is their main source of livelihood, though they have achieved greater notoriety by their piratical practice of chasing other seabirds, particularly boobies, and making them disgorge their catch, which they then retrieve in the air by amazing feats of aerial skill and precision.

As it glides tirelessly across the sky, the male of the species looks like a large black bird with a long pale bill and a barely visible dull red stripe running down its throat. However, when it wants to attract a female, its whole appearance alters dramatically; the little red gash swells and is blown up into a huge scarlet balloon. Throwing back its head and raising this astounding protuberance towards the sky, it stretches out its long wings to reveal the under-surfaces and agitates them furiously, at the same time giving vent to a prolonged, high-pitched, trilling yodel. Several males often perform together in competition to attract any female flying past, putting on a show which is unique in nature. Whether in its ecstatic courtship display or performing its aerial acrobatics, the frigate is an outstandingly spectacular bird.

The Galapagos have no less than three breeding species of booby. The name probably derives from the Spanish bobo, meaning silly or clownlike, and earned because of the booby's resemblance to a clown. While two of the three can be found on other tropical islands, their presence adds much to the ornithological interest of the Galapagos. Although their total numbers do not remotely rival those of the Peruvian offshore islands and, therefore, provide no basis for a guano industry, there are many tens of thousands breeding up and down the archipelago, and Tower Island probably

211

has the largest red-footed booby colony in the world. The red-footed nests in bushes, while the Nazca and the blue-footed nest on the ground like others of their family. It is an extraordinary experience to walk among the boobies' nesting grounds on Genovesa Island. They pay no heed at all to humans, and surround them with an eerie chorus of whistles, whoops, honks and trills, creating an atmosphere reminiscent of the strange lost world of Conan Doyle's imagination.

The Galapagos flamingo is not generally classed as such, but it is a very distinct subspecies. Like certain other Galapagos specialities, it appears to have strong affinities with those found in the Caribbean area, but in other respects it resembles South American forms. Quite apart from its interest to science, it is a bird of outstanding beauty and, with adequate protection, its rich colours and stately walk can continue to give joy to the increasing number of nature lovers who visit the islands. Its numbers have probably always been low, not more than about 500–700 in all. By Galapagos standards flamingoes are shy birds and resent disturbance, particularly in their breeding places, where they build their curious nests of mud in the very limited number of suitable shallow lagoons.

Of the world's forty-three gulls, only two breed in the Galapagos but these breed nowhere else. As a family, gulls are shore or coastal birds, and the lava gull is typical, being at home near the tide edge. It is nearly omnivorous, and is equally ready to scavenge on the beach, catch a fish in the shallows or steal an egg. With a total population of less than four hundred pairs, it may be the rarest gull in the world but there are no grounds for thinking it was more numerous in the past. In appearance it is not unlike its mainland relative, the Peruvian grey gull, being almost as black as the lava with a bright white eyelid and a striking flame-coloured gape. The value of its camouflage colouring is far from obvious as it has no enemy other than the frigate bird, which sometimes robs it, but it may be of marginal help when the bird is sitting on eggs. Certainly the lava gull is expert at concealing its solitary nest, and it was not until 1965 that the first was found. It dive-bombs intruders into its nesting territory with alarmingly low attacks but so far no casualties have been reported. A rather sedentary gull, it has never been recorded outside the Galapagos Islands.

If the lava gull is a characteristic member of its family, the swallow-tailed gull is highly untypical. It is oceanic rather than coastal, travelling vast distances over the sea in search of food. Alone among gulls, it feeds at night like an owl. A further peculiarity is that it is not a scavenger but depends for its food on fishing, chiefly for squid, which come to the surface at night. Its voice is unlike that of other gulls, and its tail is much more deeply forked, even more so than those of many terns. The swallow-tailed also has the distinction of being regarded as the most beautiful gull in the world. The mantle is a lovely shade of grey, with a much darker grey hood and white underparts, the legs and feet are pink, and the long, pointed tongue, is crimson. Its most striking feature is its very large brown eyes (for fishing at night), each surrounded by a vivid vermilion orbital ring. The long thin bill is black with a pale tip and a conspicuous white patch at the base. This patch is clearly visible to the young at the nest when the parent returns from fishing in the dark and, by pecking at it, the chick stimulates the adult to regurgitate the food it has brought. They are as beautiful in their powerful and graceful flight as in repose, their long, narrow pointed wings having black tips and an easily recognisable white triangular patch.

The swallow-tailed gull lays its single egg on the shingle, the rough lava or on cliff ledges, in a nest which is little more than a scrape. There is no summer or winter in the equatorial islands, and the gulls breed throughout most of the year. These gulls nest in loose colonies, and when breeding they are extraordinarily bold. They greet intruders with loud ungull-like cries, which specialists have broken down into a number of distinct and significant calls but which to the non-expert are simply a persistent racket. They hate to give ground if their nest is approached and will shriek and peck at a sea-lion if it gets too close to their egg. One ornithologist, Michael Harris, has seen a gull suffer a broken leg rather than make way for a big bull. Fearless as they are near their nests, they are reported to be very shy when away from them. Unlike the lava gulls, they leave the islands when they have finished breeding and wander over the ocean, particularly towards the coast of Peru.

Albatrosses are normally associated with the icy gales of the Antarctic Ocean, but, surprisingly enough, there is one species which breeds in the Galapagos within a few miles of the equatorial line. The waved albatross is found only on Hood Island; it alights on no other land in the archipelago nor elsewhere in the world, except for a small group on Ecuador's Isla de la Plata, though it roams the Pacific Ocean when not breeding. By no means the biggest member of its family, it is still a large bird, being the size of a goose and with a wingspan of 2.5 metres or so. Built for ranging over the high seas, it is an impressive spectacle as it glides above the waves, but ungainly as it waddles through the boulders and spiny scrub of Hood, a smallish, low and arid island. The waved albatross gets its name from the wavy grey lines which decorate the whole of its white underparts. Above it is brownish black and its white head and neck are lightly washed with yellow. The most striking feature is the bright yellow bill, 150 millimetres long and hooked at the end. Such a large bird, admirably adapted as it is to sailing on the high winds, is at a grievous disadvantage on land. When coming in from the sea it often tumbles over and injuries are common. In order to take off it needs a long runway; it patters along with outstretched wings over the uneven ground, striving to reach a speed at which it can become airborne. A cliff edge would be an obvious convenience for the take-off but for some reason the albatrosses frequently nest hundreds of metres inland, and so have a long and laborious trudge to reach one.

To describe the albatross as having a nest is stretching a point in its favour. The single egg, weighing about 230 grammes is simply laid on the bare ground. When hatched the chick is brooded for a fortnight, after which it is left to its own devices for most of the time. The parents return only to feed it, which is a big enough job in itself. Albatrosses have a sort of chemical plant in their stomach where they convert fish and crustaceans into oil. This enables them to stay out at sea for days on end, returning with an ample supply of liquid food which is pumped up into the chick. Feeds are few, often days apart, but enormous when they occur. One scientist, Bryan Nelson, found that a chick could take over 1.8 kilograms at a single meal lasting only a few minutes. Admittedly at the end of it the fortunate (or unfortunate) offspring, with its bulging belly, could no longer stand on its feet. High-pressure feeding goes on for week after week until, at the end of five months, the downy, chocolate-coloured chick weighs much more than either of its parents. As it emerges from downy babyhood to feathered adolescence, the youngster begins to slim and assume more aerodynamic proportions, but it will probably be thirty weeks old before it can take to the air and the ocean, and so become self-supporting. How it finds its way back to the lonely, desolate island of its birth and the only place in the vast ocean where in its turn it can breed, is one of the mysteries of migration which still calls vainly for a satisfactory answer.

These albatrosses have a remarkably elaborate courtship ritual, which they persist in long after every egg in the colony has been hatched. It is a formal 'dance' in which a number of standard movements or positions are repeated again and again, though not always in the same sequence. The two birds face one another and touch their great bills together. They weave their bills one round the other; now one of them stretches its long neck and bill vertically skywards; they cross bills as fencers cross their foils; and then one or both open their bills in a mighty gape. With variations and brief disengagements for ritualised walks, the ceremony can last for half an hour, punctuated with bill-clappering, grunts, whoops and something resembling laughter. When the excitement increases and a number of pairs join in the display, it creates a memorable sight.

With courtship, incubation period and upwards of six months spent feeding the chick, the breeding season does not leave much of the albatross's year for roaming the high seas. It is not surprising therefore that pairs do not breed every year. They are thought to breed every second or third year but, as these are long-lived birds, it will no doubt be some time before the ringing and recording operations of the Darwin station produce reliable life histories and population statistics. The interval between layings, the single egg and the probability that these albatrosses do not breed at all until they are about five years old, makes reproduction a slow process at best, and there are occasional bad years. In 1967 for instance, there were heavy rains, and even the dead-seeming shrubs on normally bone-dry Hood burst into life. However, mosquitoes also burst into life and Roger Peterson, as wide-ranging a voyager as any albatross, claimed that they were worse than the blood-sucking hordes of the Arctic tundra. Maddened by the unaccustomed insects, most of these great seabirds abandoned their eggs.

It is surprising to find an albatross breeding near the equator, but how much more so to find a penguin! The Galapagos penguin nests in a tiny area straddling the equatorial line and is accordingly the only penguin to have crossed into the northern hemisphere, though not very far. Not only is it the sole equatorial penguin, it was also the last species to be discovered, the one about which the least is known even today, and, sad to say, the rarest member of its family. That it should be one of the smallest penguins is in accordance with Bergmann's Law, which states that closely-related species tend to be biggest in the coldest areas and smallest as they approach the tropics. Thus the 40-kilogram emperor penguin breeds on the Antarctic ice and its tiny Galapagos relative on the equator. It is safe to assume that it arrived at the islands in the cool waters of the Humboldt current, which has made it easier for a cold-climate bird to adapt to this improbable habitat. Nevertheless, it remains a remarkable feat. As Robert Cushman Murphy observed: 'The species is, indeed, a monument among vertebrates to the directive or selective power of an environment, and to the fact that the filling of ecological niches is another warrant for the old law that nature abhors a vacuum.'

There is something endearing about the little penguin, so tame, so friendly, as it clambers awkwardly up the steep, wet lava, using its flippers to help its feet, hops along on the flat slabs, or plops back into the sea feet first. Lubberly on land, it is in its element under water, where its wings combine with its webbed feet to give it a pretty turn of speed. Although its wings are useless for flying, it sometimes shoots out of the water for short distances like a porpoise. Its numbers are small, perhaps two to three thousand, and probably never were very great nor ever will be, even in the best circumstances. There is little deliberate persecution nowadays but with so small a population, this delightful bird needs all the protection we can give it.

A neighbour of the penguin in the small corner of the archipelago where they both breed is an even more remarkable bird, the flightless cormorant. While the Galapagos penguin is the smallest in the world, the flightless cormorant is the largest member of its family (experts will have to explain how this fits in with Bergmann's Law). As its name implies, this cormorant's wings are useless for flying. Indeed, they no longer seem to serve any useful purpose whatever for the bird does not use them even in swimming, as the penguin does, but keeps them closely tucked in to its body, relying entirely on the powerful thrusts of its great webbed feet. A true cormorant nevertheless, on emerging from the water it stands with its wings outstretched to dry in the sun, when the short, poorly feathered remnants look like the ragged sails of a derelict windmill.

Presumably this cormorant, finding abundant food in the water around its remote island, lived more and more in the sea. With no enemies to fear on land, the ability to fly lost its selective advantage and was subordinated to skill in the water, and gradually the unused wings atrophied. The flightless cormorant is highly efficient in the water but this high degree of specialisation could lead to its extinction if its environment changes. The arrival of humans and their domestic animals could herald such a change. The late, lamented flightless dodo failed to survive human invasion.

While the penguins nest in caves and cracks that are difficult to find, the cormorants prefer flat areas of lava, open to view. There, by the edge of the sea, they build their nests of seaweed, flotsam and droppings. When a breeding bird returns from fishing, it courteously presents its blue-eyed mate with a piece of seaweed which may, or may not, be added to the nest. They are very tame and during the breeding season, at least, it would be easy enough to kill cormorants with a stick. In fact, ships' crews often amused themselves in this way. There are probably less than one thousand pairs in the Galapagos and none anywhere else.

Another and very different bird in considerable danger is the Galapagos Hawk. Although a distinct species, it is related to other birds in the genus Buteo on the mainland, most closely to the zone-tailed hawk. It must be the tamest hawk on Earth and this, of course, is its undoing. Early travellers' stories were full of hawks alighting on their guns and the ways of killing them without even using those guns. As these hawks were never regarded as a gastronomic delicacy, the killing in those days was purely for 'sport', perhaps encouraged by feelings of hostility to birds of prey. These instincts have no doubt persisted, but the arrival of settlers added the more substantial motive of protecting chickens. Formerly common, the Galapagos Hawk has lately become extinct on three of the islands where it previously bred and it survives only tenuously on the others, with a total population of less than eight hundred birds. It would be tragic if the Galapagos were to lose their only hawk and such a splendid one. The islands are surprisingly lacking in birds of prey, having only this buzzard and the two owls. There are no kites, falcons or accipiters, and no vultures. This lack of predators is no doubt largely responsible for the extraordinary tameness of the birds and beasts, just as the absence of humans, until biologically recent times, was responsible for the tameness of the Galapagos Hawk.

There are two groups of birds in the Galapagos that attract the attention of every visitor and stir excitement in the breast of every self-respecting ornithologist, the finches and the mockingbirds. Their appearance is not at all spectacular but they were the catalytic agent that started the process in Darwin's mind that led him to his revolutionary theory.

To the Europeans the mockingbirds may look like 'a sort of thrush' but to the Americans they are quite obviously 'mockers'. They differ in many ways from the North American species and from the one in the coastal region of Ecuador nearest to the islands. More importantly they differ from island to island. Until such time as the specialists can agree among themselves, if they ever do, we must leave open the question of whether there are eleven species or four species, or eleven races of a single species. The main thing is that they do differ not only from other species but from one another in size, length and shape of bill, length of leg, colour, voice and probably habits. Yet they are clearly all descended from the same ancestral stock, and have developed in different directions during long periods of isolation on the separate islands.

While there are differences of degree, it is fair to say that they are a bold, cheeky, inquisitive clan who make the thieving magpie and the jackdaw of Rheims look like timorous and incompetent amateurs. They will steal anything, anywhere, edible or not, and they are nearly omnivorous, feeding on insects, crustaceans, fruit, eggs, lizards, dead chicks and anything in a lunch packet that comes within range of their rather long, curved bills. With their longer legs, they run more and fly less than the mainland species. Mockingbirds have prospered in this harsh environment not by specialisation but by adaptability. As few forms of passerines have been able to reach and establish themselves in the Galapagos, they have enterprisingly occupied and exploited niches which, on the mainland, belong to several different species.

Few birds have had so much written about them, and probably none has made such an impact on science, as Darwin's finches. Roughly sparrow-sized and coloured black or grey-brown, they are not a very exciting group until one looks a little closer and notices the extraordinary range of shapes and sizes of their bills. Together they constitute the most remarkable living demonstration of the evolutionary principle. Most of them are sufficiently similar to suggest very strongly indeed that they are descended from a common ancestor, but at the same time they are sufficiently different in appearance and habits to be visibly members of separate species. It was Darwin's luck to have encountered this most beautiful illustration of species formation; it was his genius that enabled him to understand what he saw.

Like the mockingbirds, the finches have taken over a number of ecological niches occupied by a variety of mainland avian families which have either failed to reach or failed to establish themselves in the Galapagos archipelago. However, they have evolved along rather different lines; whereas a single species of mockingbird exploits a number of niches, the finches have become more specialised. For instance, the ground finches look very much alike, but they have developed a range of bills adapted to taking different types of seeds. At one end of the range *Geospiza fuliginosa* has a bill about the size of that of a European goldfinch and is suited to eating relatively small, soft seeds, while at the other end *Geospiza magnirostris'* bill is bigger than that of a hawfinch and it is probably the most powerful bill of any finch in the world, adapted to crushing the hardest seeds. Because of this differentiation in feeding habits, the two can live side by side. The same is true of a little group of tree finches. They all have more or less parrot-shaped bills, but these bills are sufficiently distinct to allow each to exploit a different type of food.

Other members of the family have diverged quite markedly from the typical finch pattern. One of them, *Geospiza scandens*, has a slim, tapered bill, well adapted to probing cactus flowers and pads, but otherwise it looks very much like the ground finches. There are no tits in the Galapagos and their ecological role has been taken over by one of Darwin's finches, which feeds and behaves in much the same way as a tit. Similarly another member of the family has occupied the niche of the warbler and vireo. With its slender pointed bill, it flits restlessly around in search of insects. It has not only come to behave like a warbler but actually to look very much like one, so much so that Darwin at first had difficulty in believing that it belonged to the finch family.

Perhaps even more remarkable and certainly more spectacular in its behaviour, is *Cactospiza pallida*, commonly called the woodpecker finch. Again because they are absent from the islands, this finch has occupied the niche filled elsewhere by the nuthatches and the woodpecker. Its strong, sharp bill enables it to dig into soft wood, like a small woodpecker, and open up insect burrows. However, from this point onwards the finch is at a disadvantage because it lacks the long, barbed tongue with which most true woodpeckers winkle out the exposed insect from the bottom of the hole. The finch has largely overcome this disability by the extraordinary device of using a tool. Having uncovered its prey, it looks for a cactus spine or a thin twig. Holding this in its bill, it prods the insect until it moves or is otherwise brought within range. It is most unusual for a bird to use a tool but this finch is astounding and virtually unique among birds in that it is also a tool-maker. It may pick up a fallen spine but, if none is conveniently available, it will break one off the nearest cactus, or it may take a twig and break it to the right size and shape for its particular purpose. This shows undeniably that the bird is not just acting instinctively but that it is using its intelligence to relate cause and effect.

More than anything else it was this remarkable group of finches that so deeply impressed Darwin and inspired his much quoted lines: 'Seeing this gradation and diversity of structure in one small, intimately related group of birds, one might really fancy that from an original paucity of birds in this archipelago, one species had been taken and modified for different ends.'

Bibliography

Angermeyer, J.. *My Father's Island*, (London 2003)

Anon. *Colección de Documentos Ineditos de Indias. Voyage of Diego de Rivadeneira to the Galapagos*, Vol. XII, pp. 538–44.

Beebe, Charles William. *Galapagos, World's End*, (New York, 1924.) *The Arcturus Adventure*, (New York, 1926.)

Burney, James. *History of the Buccaneers of America*. (London, 1891.)

Byron, George Anson, Baron. *Voyage of HMS* Blonde *to the Sandwich Islands in the years 1824–25*. (London, 1826.)

Colnett, Captain James. *A Voyage to the South Atlantic and round Cape Horn into the Pacific Ocean, for the purpose of extending the Spermacetic whale fisheries*. (London, 1798.)

Conway, Ainslie and Frances. *The Enchanted Islands*. (New York, 1947.)

Cowley, Ambrose. *Voyage Around the World*. (London, 1699.)

Dampier, William. *A New Voyage Round the World*. (London, 1697.)

Darwin, Charles Robert. *A Naturalist's Voyage Round the World in HMS* Beagle. (London, 1839.)

Charles Darwin's Diary of the Voyage of HMS Beagle. Ed. by Nora Barlow. (Cambridge, 1933.)

De Roy, T.. *Galapagos: Islands Born of Fire*, (London 2008.)

Fitter J., Fitter D. & Hosking D.. Wildlife of the Galapagos (London 2007.)

Fitzroy, Admiral Robert. *Narrative of the Surveying Voyages of His Majesty's ships* Adventure *and* Beagle, Vol. II. (London, 1839. 3

Vols.)

Foreign Office, Great Britain. *Peace Handbooks prepared under direction of Historical Section*, Vol. XXII. (London, 1920.)

Forester, Cecil Scott. *The Age of Fighting Sail.* (London, 1968.)

Grant, P. R. *Ecology and Evolution of Darwin's Finches.* (Princeton 2000.)

Grant, Von Hagen, Victor Wolfgang. *Ecuador the Unknown.* (New York, 1940.) *Ecuador and the Galapagos Islands.* (University of Oklahoma Press, 1949.)

Hall, Basil, RN. *Extracts from a Journal written on the coasts of Chile, Peru and Mexico, Edinburgh.* (1824. 2 Vols.)

Horwell, D. & Oxford P. *Galapagos Wildlife: A Visitor's Guide.* (Bradt 2005.)

Jackson, M. H. *Galapagos: A Natural History.* (Calgary 1993.)

Keynes, R. D. *The* Beagle *Record.* (Cambridge, 1979.)

Larrea, Carlos Manuel. *El Archipiélago de Colón.* (Quito, 1958.)

Manning, William R. *Diplomatic Correspondence of the United States. Inter-American affairs, 1831–1860,* Vol. VI. (Washington, 1935. 12 Vols.)

Markham, C. R. 'Discovery of the Galapagos Islands', *Proceedings of the Royal Geographical Society,* Vol. XIV. (1892, pp. 314–16.)

Markham, Captain A. H.. 'A visit to the Galapagos Islands in 1880', Proceedings of the Royal Geographical Society, new series, Vol. II. (1880, pp. 742–55.)

Means, Philip Ainsworth. *Ancient Civilizations of the Andes.* (New York, 1931.)

Melville, Herman. *The Encantadas or Enchanted Isles . . ., with an introduction, critical epilogue, and bibliographical notes by Victor Wolfgang von Hagen.* (San Francisco, 1940.)

Mielche, Hakon. *Let's See if the World is Round.* (London, 1938.)

Morrell, Benjamin. *A Narrative of four voyages to the South Sea, North and South Pacific Ocean.* (New York, 1832.)

Nicholls, H. *Life and Loves of a Conservation Icon.* (London 2006.)

Ortelius. *Theatrum Orbis Terrarum.* (Amsterdam, 1570.)

Parks, E. Taylor, and Rippy, J. Fred. 'The Galapagos Islands, a Neglected Phase of American Strategic Diplomacy', *The Pacific Historical Review*, Vol. IX, No. 1. (March 1940, pp. 37–45.)

Porter, David. *Journal of a Cruise made to the Pacific Ocean by Captain David Porter in the US Frigate Essex in the years 1812, 1813, and 1814, Philadelphia.* (1815. 2 Vols.)

Ritter, Friedrich. 'Adam and Eve in the Galapagos', *The Atlantic Monthly*, Vol. CXLVIII. (October 1931, pp. 409–18.)

Als Robinson auf Galapagos. (Leipzig, 1935.)

'Eve calls it a Day', *The Atlantic Monthly*, Vol. CXLVIII. (December 1931, pp. 733–43.)

'Satan Walks in the Garden'. *The Atlantic Monthly*, Vol. CXLVIII. (November 1931, pp. 565–75.)

Robinson, William Albert. *Voyage to Galapagos.* (London, 1936.)

Rogers, Captain Woodes. *A Cruising Voyage round the World.* (London, 1709.)

Slevin, Joseph R. '*The Galapagos Islands: A History of their Exploration*'. Proceedings of the California Academy of Sciences. (1959.)

Strauch, Dore. *Satan Came to Eden.* (New York and London 1935.)

Treherne, John. *The Galapagos Affair.* (London, 1983.)

Thornton, Ian. *Darwin's Islands: A Natural History of the Galapagos.* (New York, 1971.)

Wafer, Lionel. *A new voyage and description of the Isthmus of America.* (London, 1699.)

Wittmer, Margret. *Floreana.* (London, 1931.)

Wolf, Theodor. *Geografia y Geologia del Ecuador.* (Leipzig, 1892.)

Wycherley, George. *Buccaneers of the Pacific.* (London, 1929.)

ELAND

61 Exmouth Market, London EC1R 4QL
Tel: 020 7833 0762   Fax: 020 7833 4434
Email: info@travelbooks.co.uk

Eland was started in 1982 to revive great travel books
that had fallen out of print. Although the list has diversified
into biography and fiction, it is united by a quest to define the
spirit of place. These are books for travellers, and for readers who aspire
to explore the world but who are also content to travel in their own
minds.

Eland books open out our understanding of other
cultures, interpret the unknown and reveal different environments
as well as celebrating the humour and occasional horrors of travel. We
take immense trouble to select only the most readable
books and therefore many readers collect the entire series.

All our books are printed on fine, pliable, cream-coloured paper.
Most are still gathered in sections by our printer and sewn as well
as glued, almost unheard of for a paperback book these days.
This gives larger margins in the gutter, as well as
making the books stronger.

You will find a very brief description of all our books on the
following pages. Extracts from each and every one of them can be
read on our website, at www.travelbooks.co.uk. If you would
like a free copy of our catalogue, please telephone, email
or write to us (details above).

ELAND

'*One of the very best travel lists*' WILLIAM DALRYMPLE

Memoirs of a Bengal Civilian
JOHN BEAMES
*Sketches of nineteenth-century India
painted with the richness of Dickens*

Jigsaw
SYBILLE BEDFORD
*An intensely remembered autobiographical
novel about an inter-war childhood*

A Visit to Don Otavio
SYBILLE BEDFORD
*The hell of travel and the Eden of arrival
in post-war Mexico*

Journey into the Mind's Eye
LESLEY BLANCH
*An obsessive love affair with Russia and
one particular Russian*

Japanese Chronicles
NICOLAS BOUVIER
*Three decades of intimate experiences
throughout Japan*

The Way of the World
NICOLAS BOUVIER
Two men in a car from Serbia to Afghanistan

Persia: through writers' eyes
ED. DAVID BLOW
*Guidebooks for the mind: a selection
of the best travel writing on Iran*

The Devil Drives
FAWN BRODIE
*Biography of Sir Richard Burton,
explorer, linguist and pornographer*

Turkish Letters
OGIER DE BUSBECQ
*Eyewitness history at its best:
Istanbul during the reign of Suleyman
the Magnificent*

My Early Life
WINSTON CHURCHILL
*From North-West Frontier to Boer War
by the age of twenty-five*

Sicily: through writers' eyes
ED. HORATIO CLARE
*Guidebooks for the mind: a selection
of the best travel writing on Sicily*

A Square of Sky
JANINA DAVID
*A Jewish childhood in the Warsaw
ghetto and hiding from the Nazis*

Chantemesle
ROBIN FEDDEN
*A lyrical evocation of childhood
in Normandy*

Croatia: through writers' eyes
ED. FRANKOPAN, GOODING & LAVINGTON
*Guidebooks for the mind: a selection
of the best travel writing on Croatia*

Viva Mexico!
CHARLES FLANDRAU
A traveller's account of life in Mexico

Travels with Myself and Another
MARTHA GELLHORN
*Five journeys from hell by a great
war correspondent*

The Weather in Africa
MARTHA GELLHORN
*Three novellas set amongst the
white settlers of East Africa*

The Last Leopard
DAVID GILMOUR
*The biography of Giuseppe di Lampedusa,
author of* The Leopard

Walled Gardens
ANNABEL GOFF
An Anglo-Irish childhood

Africa Dances
GEOFFREY GORER
*The magic of indigenous culture
and the banality of colonisation*

Ask Sir James
MICHAELA REID
The life of Sir James Reid,
personal physician to Queen Victoria

A Funny Old Quist
EVAN ROGERS
A gamekeeper's passionate evocation
of a now-vanished English rural lifestyle

Meetings with Remarkable Muslims
ED. ROGERSON & BARING
A collection of contemporary travel
writing that celebrates cultural difference
and the Islamic world

Marrakesh: through writers' eyes
ED. ROGERSON & LAVINGTON
Guidebooks for the mind: a selection
of the best travel writing on Marrakesh

Turkish Aegean: through writers' eyes
ED. RUPERT SCOTT
Guidebooks for the mind: a selection
of the best travel writing on Turkey

Valse des Fleurs
SACHEVERELL SITWELL
A day in St Petersburg in 1868

Living Poor
MORITZ THOMSEN
An American's encounter with
poverty in Ecuador

Hermit of Peking
HUGH TREVOR-ROPER
The hidden life of the scholar
Sir Edmund Backhouse

The Law
ROGER VAILLAND
The harsh game of life played in
the taverns of southern Italy

Bangkok
ALEC WAUGH
The story of a city

The Road to Nab End
WILLIAM WOODRUFF
The best selling story of poverty and
survival in a Lancashire mill town

The Village in the Jungle
LEONARD WOOLF
A dark novel of native villagers struggling
to survive in colonial Ceylon

Death's Other Kingdom
GAMEL WOOLSEY
The tragic arrival of civil war in an
Andalucian village in 1936

The Ginger Tree
OSWALD WYND
A Scotswoman's love and survival
in early twentieth-century Japan

Poetry of Place series

London: Poetry of Place
ED. BARING & ROGERSON
A poetry collection like the city itself, full of
grief, irony and delight

Andalus: Poetry of Place
ED. TED GORTON
Moorish songs of love and wine

Venice: Poetry of Place
ED. HETTY MEYRIC HUGHES
Eavesdrop on the first remembered glimpses
of the city, and meditations on her history

Desert Air: Poetry of Place
ED. MUNRO & ROGERSON
On Arabia, deserts and the Orient of
the imagination

Istanbul: Poetry of Place
ED. ATES ORGA
Poetry from her long history, from paupers to
sultans, natives and visitors alike

The Ruins of Time
ED. ANTHONY THWAITE
Sized to fit any purse or pocket, this is just the
book to complement a picnic amongst the
ruins of time